The Greatest Thing You'll Ever Learn

Dudley E. Flood, Ed. D.

authorHOUSE®

AuthorHouse™
1663 Liberty Drive, Suite 200
Bloomington, IN 47403
www.authorhouse.com
Phone: 1-800-839-8640

First published by AuthorHouse 4/15/2009

ISBN: 978-1-4389-5702-9 (sc)

Printed in the United States of America
Bloomington, Indiana

This book is printed on acid-free paper.

ACKNOWLEDGEMENTS

I HAVE LONG HESITATED TO WRITE this book, because I could not convince myself that I had something to say that would be of general interest sufficient to justify the effort. However, after hearing from my family and particularly my wife, Barbara, that I should do so, I resolved to share these thoughts in the hope that someone would be inspired to live life more fully, to enjoy the journey more thankfully, to serve humanity more completely, and to laugh more heartily.

I thank the many friends who have asked, "Why don't you write a book?" I always took this to be a rhetorical question until recently when it donned on me that I will not be making talks forever, and some of my talks have given comfort and even enjoyment to many and inspiration to others.

I am grateful to Craig Phillips, the first "boss" that I had who encouraged me to engage in public thought, which is the basis of public speaking. I am grateful to Undean Jones who taught me the English language in great depth when I was a high school student, and to Charles Ray who furthered my love for the language at North Carolina College at Durham, (now North Carolina Central University). I am eternally indebted to the thousands of persons who have been my audiences over the past forty years. Most of all, I am thankful to God for the gift of utterance that I hope that I have used to His glory.

Contents

Chapter I

THE GREATEST THING
YOU'LL EVER LEARN

AS FAR BACK AS I can recall, I have had a fascination with poetry and music. During my early childhood, I memorized the lyrics of scores of songs and the words of tens of poems. In every one of them, I thought that I saw someone that I knew as the leading character or as the person about whom the poem or song had been written. While I recognized this as being my own fantasy, it nevertheless had a profound effect on the way that I saw the world and the way that I defined my place therein.

My favorite singer during my childhood was Nat "King" Cole, and my favorite song among his many great offerings was a song titled NATURE BOY. That was the song that was written by Eden Ahbez which I imagined was written about me. Its lyrics began, "There was a boy, a very strange, enchanted boy". I truly imagined that I was "strange" in the sense that I did not in my mind fit the mold for my generation. I always preferred the company of persons older than I, and I most enjoyed activities that were not embraced readily by my chronological peers. I did not think of myself

1

as "enchanted" but I would reason that this characteristic was something that I would later develop as I matured.

The next line, "They say he wandered very far, very far, over land and sea" was clearly speaking of me. The farthest that I had been from my hometown of Winton, North Carolina was to Franklin, Virginia which was some thirty miles away, but I had seen the world through books. The trips that I took to far away places lived with and in me as clearly as if I had physically experienced them.

"A little shy, and sad of eye, but very wise was he." That was the me that I saw. I defined wise as being the ability to reason and to make sound decisions. I said to myself, that is a good goal to set for your life and I did set that as a goal. The next few lines were a lead-in to the real kicker that charted my course in life…"and then one day—one magic day he passed my way—and while we spoke of many things, fools and kings, this he said to me".—At this point Nat Cole had my undivided attention. My interest had peeked to a point of knowing that whatever comes next is the ultimate directive to the formula for a great, productive, successful life experience. And indeed that was true beyond a shadow of doubt. He continued and concluded—"The greatest thing you'll ever learn is JUST TO LOVE AND BE LOVED IN RETURN." That is the most telling piece of advice that I have yet received.

This book is dedicated to that principle. Knowing how to love and be loved is a learned skill. If developed early in life, it can be a source of enormous satisfaction throughout the rest of our days. However, it is not too late to develop and to begin to practice that principle at whatever point in life you are willing to make that commitment. In my career as an educator and as a public speaker, I have tried always to model the act of loving. If I have been successful, the proof can be found in the fact that all my former students can say with conviction that they have truly had the experience of having been loved. So can my friends and above all, my family members.

I am including in this book excerpts from several of my favorite presentations and from some of the essays and articles that I have written over the years. While each of my presentations has several versions, depending on the setting and audience, each is built on some generic considerations, but with the single theme that is the title of this book. There is no greater truth that the well worn cliché," people don't care how much you know until they know how much you care".

Chapter II

THE SILENT CRISIS

I BEGIN EACH DAY BY READING the morning newspaper, hoping that today will be the day that there is an announcement of a declaration of a truce between the forces of good and evil; of war and peace; of poverty and affluence; of the powerful and the powerless; of the employed and the unemployed; of the government and the governed; of the schooled and the unschooled; and indeed of any or all of the elements of polarization within our otherwise great society. Though I continue to read with hope, I rarely find reason to think that the present generation of leaders have profited from the experiences of those who came before them. There appears to be a trend toward recapitulation in ways that we seldom discuss. In fact, to make mention of such matters is now seen as lacking appreciation for all the progress that our nation has enjoyed.

Many of our present day challenges can be traced back to our having not completed the course of actions that were bearing incremental success. In our impatience for solutions to issues that had developed over centuries, we dismantled strategies without replacing them with better strategies. The logical consequences of such action is that not only have these issues re-surfaced, though in different forms, but that now we lack confidence in our ability to address them successfully, so we act as if they did not exist.

Possibly the most visible indication of this trend can be found in the field of education. The time honored practice of assigning a cluster of students to a teacher and directing all available resources at helping that teacher to be successful in the education of those students has all but been abandoned. There can be found as many justifications for this abandonment as are needed to make us feel better about having done so, but the will to reverse this trend still eludes us. It may be useful for us to revisit some of the factors that produced successful students in schools that had few of the modern conveniences, none of the technology now available to us, and dramatically less sophisticated management structures than are common in today's schools. Yet, our children learned the academic offerings, developed character and most became productive citizens.

My observations are not based only on my experiences as an educator, though I have spent more than fifty years in that role. Beyond that fact, I have provided training to educators in more than 3,500 settings, in all of the United States except South Dakota and Montana at the time of this writing. I have also trained personnel in more than ten locations in Canada, in Germany and in Bermuda. The conclusions that I have reached are based on interactions with these and other professionals as well as on my own experiences.

Many studies have been done on the matter of school improvement, and most have concluded that two elements are in need of repair; those being the art of teaching and the art of providing leadership in the school setting. Some have gone so far as to propose strategies for improving each of these components. Most have concluded that in order to determine whether progress is being made in those areas, we should give all the children a norm referenced standardized achievement test based on what society has determined that students should know at a given point in their educational journey. Should they fail to achieve that amount of progress, we then conclude that the teacher has fallen short or that the leadership is inadequate, but we rarely offer a definitive plan for rectifying either of these conditions.

Some theorize that we should test the educators more rigidly and replace those whose students are not performing up to expectations. However, as the supply of available educators has dwindled, this has become a less viable option. Others offer that more focus should be given to strengthening those personnel that are in the workforce, but few have managed to appropriate the time for that sort of activity to take place. Other efforts are being implemented that have promise, but many of these require funding that is not available to the average school district. In short, the progress is slower in the places of greatest need because the necessary human and fiscal resources are not in line with the proposed strategies for improvement.

What we do know is that success in any walk of life is predicated on there being clear definition of the desired outcome and the creation of a set of steps toward that end. The difficult part is the defining of the desired outcome for all students because of the various elements of society that have a vested interest in the end product. Some have a very narrow perception of what constitutes a successful educational experience while others have an unrealistic view of what is possible to achieve in a setting such as school. One way to cover all these bases is that of asking ourselves to focus on the elements of success that we can agree upon and teaching toward the development of these elements. For me, this would require that we concentrate on five sets of proficiencies which may be arrived at in various ways, but which would constitute the desired outcome from the formal education that we provide for all students.

The word proficiency is more definitive than competency. The latter suggests performance at a remedial or functional level, whereas proficiency suggests that one has reached a level of mastery that makes certain actions common practice. At that level, best practice becomes common practice.

The first goal must be that all students become intellectually proficient. Indicators of this proficiency are that the student will be able to write and speak a language with clarity and with understanding; to compute and use numbers and to understand the language of mathematics; to reason independently and to use his or her reasoning ability to address day to day decision making; and to have an appreciation for and tendency toward life long learning. With this goal in mind, educators might discover that various curricular offerings may lead to that defined outcome, but the offerings need not be the same for all students so long as the outcome is achieved to a verifiable level. No specific timetable can be mandated for all achievers as students learn at differing rates and speeds, but the outcome must be similar for all students.

To achieve this goal for all students, it is necessary for educators to truly believe that all students, well taught, can acquire an acceptable level of intellectual proficiency. It is common to find an expression of this belief written in the mission statement of a school on even becoming a central theme of the school's planning process. It is less common to see this belief reflected in the way teaching is carried out or even in the way that teaching is evaluated. One deterrent to implementing this objective is the fact that much of the outcome is difficult to measure. Whether one speaks well is observable, but hardly measurable by objective means. Whether one understands basic concepts of math can best be determined through classroom demonstration by the student and by practical application of these principles to real life situations. Such a process may yield less that desirable test scores for reasons having nothing to do with ones understanding of the concepts in question. In this way, the various elements in intellectual growth are interdependent and are best nurtured in a seamless paradigm. We cannot hope to achieve a desired result at one level when there is no continuity from one learning setting to the next. Even when we sequence curriculum offerings but fail to maintain philosophical continuity, productivity is decreased.

In the traditional school setting that most of us experienced fifty years ago, a teacher had multiple opportunities to interact with a given student. One of my most successful students frequently reminds me that I first taught him science in the fifth grade; later was his homeroom teacher and had him all day in the eighth grade; followed him to high school where I was his football coach and his American Government teacher. During his middle school years, I had been his Boy Scout Master and his Explorer Scout Advisor. It should come as no surprise that my influence on his development was move significant than it could have been had I seen him for only forty-eight minutes a day. His intellectual development was a product of constant interaction between him and someone that he knew had a personal stake in his progress. Naturally, there were other influences in his life; some good and some not so desirable, but the closeness of the teacher-student relationship gave the advantage to the teacher to be successful in exerting a positive influence.

Let it be understood that the teaching act is at the heart of academic progress, but that this act does not end at the classroom door. When a teacher models a visible respect for intellectual pursuit and celebrates the achievement of every student in that direction, the results are more likely to be positive. Educators who demonstrate a love for learning and who evidence a joy in teaching have a decisive advantage over the person who grudgingly goes through the motion of instructing with no visible interest in the development of the student. The least capable of students can sense whether he or she is valued as a person and viewed as a potential learner by a given teacher. One philosopher once remarked, "We are all children of God, but silk makes all the difference".

We have learned that young people will excel at whatever a society prizes and celebrates. The evidence of this truth can be found in the abundance of excellence in our sports programs throughout the nation. We hold major celebrations when our teams have won championships, but minor celebrations when our youth have excelled academically. We have unconsciously created a climate in which some youths are not proud of their academic success, and many will go to great lengths to obscure the fact that they are intellectually proficient. As a rule, when two teenaged students are engaged in conversation and only one of them knows the definition of a word, the one who is most embarrassed is the one that knows and he of she is likely to revert to the conversational level of the one who does not know. The obvious challenge for our society is to validate the value of intellectuality and to make it more fashionable for our youth to acquire and to demonstrate that trait.

A second acquisition of the successful person is social proficiency. There appears to be a great reduction in the emphasis that society places of social behavior in the learning environment; yet anti-social behavior carries the greatest set of penalties that I have witnessed during my fifty years of teaching. We frequently lament the high expulsion rate and the high dropout rate among present day youth. Each of these factors can be directly attributed to the inability of youth to become compatible to the school environment and to interact successfully and acceptably with others. Rarely is the lack of innate ability to learn at the root of inappropriate behavior. The greater cause is the lack of a sense of self-worth and the tendency to act out of the frustrations that this condition promotes.

When a specific priority is placed on the teaching of approved social behavior, student progress in other areas is likely to be enhanced. Great teachers equate those teachings to the act of reducing the barriers to learning. Those who believe such teachings to be a waste of time or to not fall within their responsibility, or even who recognize that there is not a "test" required on the affective domain do themselves and their students a great disservice. The evidence will appear in all walks of life, including in the school setting, that a person is grasping the importance of social skills such as gratification delay, appreciation for differences, positive self-esteem and unselfishness. These traits when acquired at an early age tend to grow with maturation of the individual and become an intricate part of the students' plan for success in life.

In addition to the aforementioned proficiencies, the person who would achieve the greatest level of success must have a realist understanding of our economic system. It is unlikely that complete economic proficiency can be achieved through being exposed to a half unit of the study of economics, generally taken as an elective to satisfy graduation requirements. In a nation in which there is no separation between the political system and the economic system, to not understand one of these is to be victimized by both.

Many of the struggles between races and classes are economic battles. Economic resources and the control thereof are the greatest source of power in our society. To not control financial resources is to be powerless in any real sense of success in our society. There was a period in our history during which power was decided by the ownership of land. During the industrial revolution, we moved away from that concept to equating power with the control of the means of production. In the face of this assumption, labor unions were developed to protect the powerless worker from the powerful boss. This activity created the illusion of power for the lay person, but what it actually did was to shift power from the owners of industry to the controllers of labor. In either case, the class at the bottom remained at the bottom, and the class at the top was joined by a few people who were successful in controlling the masses below them.

The modern trend has become that of personal empowerment through acquiring a proficiency in any particular arena and in knowing how to market that product. In this county, one can acquire an extra-ordinary amount of wealth from virtually anything at which they excel and which is not commonplace. There is no accounting for the way in which we place value on a product or on a service. Some years ago, a company made a fortune selling pet rocks. Some musical and dramatic performers totally devoid of visible talent have become icons in their respective domains. Some more talented persons have failed to realize economic success due to their inability to convince the consuming public that theirs was a valuable and desirable commodity. There is a five step process that if followed will greatly increase the likelihood that one will gain some measure of economic security. These steps, in order, are:

1. Settle on something that you like to do so well that you would do it without charge were you able to do so. It is unlikely that you will become proficient at something that you have no love for doing. It is possible that your love for applying your skill will increase as your ability in that area increases. In whatever way you come to that end, your vocation must become your avocation if you are to maximize your capability in that area.

2. Restrict your focus to that one area and work at it until you become identified so closely with that area that people think first of you when they think of that area. Whatever the area of your focus, the best marketing tool is word of mouth advertising from people who know first hand of your service or product. Your name or product must become a part of the routine daily discussions in which people regularly engage. There is no area in which this principle is not

applicable. If you are a great teacher, students regularly discuss you with their parents and other students. If you are a great physician, people regularly recommend you to their friends. If you run an excellent business, people boast about being your customer. If you are an excellent minister, people join your church because those who are already members extol your virtues.

3. Learn to make money by applying your talents in your chosen field. Learn the worth of your services and examine the market for them. Compare the value of your product or service with similar services and products and understand what sets you apart from the ordinary variety of these services or products. Learn to present your product or service in the most positive light without being overbearing. Always leave the decision to the consumer of the service. People generally conclude that any item that must be "hyped" is lacking in value or that item would have spoken for itself. The most attractive advertisement that I have ever seen was one which a company in Raleigh used to promote, "we will do good work, at a profit if we can, at a loss if we must, but we WILL do good work."

4. Begin to associate with people who have similar interests and aims for their life's work. One of the surest ways to fail is to surround yourself with people who have no appreciation for what you are trying to accomplish. It is very difficult to achieve great heights without the validation and affirmation of significant others in your life. Remember, you always have a choice with regard to with whom you associate.

5. Diversify your customer base. If you are a teacher and are very good with "bright" students, can you become equally effective in teaching less bright students? If you are an entertainer and "rap" is your

medium, can you hold and audience who has no appreciation for that art form? It not, you become extinct when it becomes extinct. If you are a medical doctor, are you attuned to the newer methods of treatment for the ailments that are common to your patients? By expanding your capacity, you also expand your client base.

These five directives are not intended to be the total pattern of our pathway to economic success. They are merely injected here as examples of a different way to think about developing economic proficiency as we work with our students. The effective teacher will create ways of infusing these principles into discussions, no matter what subject matter he or she is charged with teaching.

Another equally important need in moving successfully into adulthood is that of understanding our political system. This is the system that distributes opportunity throughout our society. When talent and opportunity are present in the same environment, success is more likely to occur.

The vital ingredient of power rests in the hands of those who know how to access the political system. It is common for poorly positioned people to create avenues that give the illusion of having power but who control nothing of value. Street gangs have been organized to control a territory, but in actuality dispensed no valued product. Clubs and organizations have been formed to create positions of status for their designated leaders, but impacted no one else in any positive manner. Such superficial structures may fill our innate need to be a part of something, but do not necessarily give us power.

Power is by definition the ability to control a desired commodity. The two elements on which to focus are control and desirable. You may own all the sand in a desert, but if no one wants your sand, you have no power through controlling that commodity. Conversely, you may own a very highly prized product but if you lack the independence to distribute it, you still lack real power.

The most reliable source of power is knowledge. This commodity is one which you can distribute at your discretion. If you are known to possess it, others will seek you out in their quest to obtain it. It is a dynamic force which increases with time and experience.

In our organized political structure, we engage in the control of resources through our voting pattern and our vocal interchange with those whom we elect to represent our views. Yet, it is common for there to be less than half the registered voters to actually cast a ballot in any election at any level. We as a society frequently fail to express our desires when it matters, but are quick to express displeasure at the sub-par performance of an elected official. However, given the opportunity to do so, we are just as likely to return the non-performing person to office at the next election. One reason that this cycle is so predictable is that we become dismissive about matters that we are convinced that we cannot control. We respond by not bothering to become involved. The only thing that a non-responsive leader needs to be continued in a powerful position is for the clear thinking population to do nothing.

Our schools provide an ideal setting in which to teach both the value of and the art of effective political involvement. Such involvement must extend beyond the act of serving on the student council or on committees that govern student life on campus. We must also expose students to the greater arena of political activity that affects their welfare. Each year, schools in our nation graduate enough potential voters who, if they were to act in unison, could virtually sway any election in their respective communities. Most often, these graduates take no interest in such matters until they are well established in their careers and have started their families. For many, the trend of non-involvement has become a way of life that followers them into adulthood. Hence, we continue to see leadership elected by twenty or thirty percent of the population.

Finally, our youth are in dire need of developing spiritual proficiencies. We who work in the field of education have been socialized to defer to the faith community for the teaching of core values, and to the home for the inculcation of morality. To assume that school has no legitimate role in spiritual development is to deny the force that models and practices have in human development. The classroom is a setting in which a student has been conditioned to learn. We know that learning is concomitant; that is to say we learn more than one thing at a time. For example, while a student is learning math, he may also be learning to detest math. While she is learning a language, she may be developing an attitude toward the use of language. These developments are both cognitive and affective. Interestingly, the area that receives more opportunity for independent development may be the affective, because it may be practiced more freely in society. If the "in" thing to do is to speak slang or a dialect, the opportunity to practice the use of formal language is severely limited.

How, then, does ones spiritual development offset such influences? It begins with a clear definition of self that is inclusive of positive behaviors. The instilling of these behaviors begins within a structured environment that defines and reinforces acceptable behavior. Our modern trend toward instituting punitive measures to curb antisocial behavior has proven to be less effective than the tried and true method of instilling desirable values through inculcation. The latter plan requires that there be general agreement among all the dispensers of influence as to what constitutes inappropriate behavior. Further, all have the permissive mandate from society to unilaterally afford guidance to all who are seen as practicing behavior outside the social norms. When adults feel it to be a moral imperative for them to guide all children's behavior, they create a seamless atmosphere of care for the welfare of all that results in a more disciplined generation. Eventually, this guided discipline results in self-direction which is the ultimate enhancer of success.

The end result of a well executed plan for developing a spiritual proficiency is that the individual will have a spiritual gyroscope that dictates behavior and provides balance between appropriate and inappropriate behavior. It creates a conscience within the individual that requires little monitoring from without, because the force of personal desire to behave properly overpowers the urge to be fashionably inappropriate.

The question that we face as a society is that of whether we are serious about assuring the success of every individual. I believe that the means for doing so are readily available to us. Were we to muster the will to deploy our talents and considerable resources in that direction, we could certainly reduce the probability that the next generation of our citizens would experience a less desirable quality of life than that which we have enjoyed. The words of the late Dr .Ronald Edmonds are as true today as when he first wrote them in 1978 when he said "We can, whenever and wherever we choose, successfully teach all children whose schooling is of interest to us. We already know more than we need to do that. Whether or not we do it must finally depend on how we feel about the fact that we haven't so far."

Chapter III

LEARNING TO LOVE YOURSELF

THE SECOND GREAT COMMANDMENT IN the Holy Bible is "Thou shall love thy neighbor as thyself." The essence of this directive is that the paradigm for loving others is found in the way that we love ourselves. Love for self begins with respect for self. Love for others begins with respect for others. Love is a deeper manifestation of our person than is "like". We are called to love persons that we do not particularly like. Generally, our likes are driven by our being able to approve of someone's behavior. Love, on the other hand, is given unconditionally, without respect to our approval or disapproval of the behavior of others. It is predicated on the deeply rooted belief that though we are imperfect beings and though we all are capable of falling short of the expectations of others, we are nonetheless worthy of love simply by our being human.

Given our bent toward imperfection, love is generally preceded by forgiveness. My first lesson in forgiveness was in learning to forgive myself for my own short comings. My knowledge of my own transgressions makes it necessary for me to continue to have conversations with myself daily. In these conversations, I do not rationalize away my imperfections, but rather, I acknowledge them to myself and commit myself to a plan for reconciliation with anyone that may have been affected by my behavior. This plan always involves seeking their forgiveness. It is not required that they utter the words "I forgive you" though that is certainly a desirable end. More importantly is the fact that we are able to mend our fractured relationship and restore our mutual respect. When that takes place, I can more easily forgive myself. However, if my genuine attempt at reconciliation does not bear fruit, I then can forgive myself on the basis of that effort. I will resolve to continue that effort without ceasing, using every reasonable opportunity to do so, but having forgiven myself empowers me to move on in a more productive way than would be the case were I to continue to self-flagellate over a single misdeed or poor choice that I have made.

Forgiveness of others is less difficult for us after we have acknowledged our own human frailty. It is unreasonable to set a higher standard for others than we set for ourselves. It is easier for us to accept that others are capable of error knowing that so are we. Having forgiven another does not free us from the responsibility to avoid situations that are likely grounds for further conflict. The old expression "forgive and forget" may be misleading if one interprets that to mean "business as usual". Rather, we must learn from every experience and we must apply this learning in charting the course of future interactions with an individual. If you have told me a lie or have lied on me, I can forgive you for either, but I will not dismiss the possibility that you may not be a suitable confidant with whom I entrust my most personal dealings. If you have stolen from me or others, I can forgive you, but it would be a while before I would select you as the administrator of my estate or bestow on you power of attorney should I become incapacitated. There would have to be some compelling evidence that you had made a value shift or a moral transformation before

I would subject myself to the possible consequence of behavior that you have demonstrated in the past.

The door must remain open for individuals to re-establish their credibility, but it does not suggest to me that forgiveness removes one from scrutiny. There is no relationship between loving and blind acceptance of poor behavior. Love the individual but reject the inappropriate behavior. This same rule applies to self and to others.

One of the tools that I find helpful in forgiving myself and others is that of developing a greater understanding of why we behave as we do. This understanding is not used to excuse the behavior but rather as a basis for developing a strategy for dealing with that particular individual. There is a field of thinking that asserts that we are prone to respond to life's situations based on the stimuli that we received as a child. The manner in which we formed our way of thinking about certain situations may become "drivers" of our adult behavior. No one "driver" can frame our total behavior pattern, but when taken in relationship to other "drivers", we may be able to see more clearly why we behave as we do. To illustrate this point, I will cite five "drivers" from my own developmental experience and the impact that each has had on my person.

First there was the "be perfect" driver. During my youth, I rarely got the feeling that I had done something well enough. In an effort to encourage me to achieve, my teachers would say things like "you are not using all of your ability". When I thought that I had done something quite well, they were likely to say, "That is good, but you can improve it" by doing thus and so. When I was certain that I had behaved well, someone was sure to offer me advice on how I might have behaved even better. If I expressed my thoughts, I was told that I talked too much. If I failed to express my thoughts, I was told that I was being too withdrawn. The overall message that I received from all of this excellent but sometimes conflicting advice was that I could be nothing less than perfect if I were to be accepted by others. This was a convoluted conclusion to have drawn, but it still had a profound impact on my behavior. More will be said about that later.

Next was the "try harder" driver. Most of the adults that were a part of my development appeared to believe that if one failed at something, it was because he or she had not tried hard enough. If I or one of my classmates did not grasp a concept in some of our subject matter, we were generally admonished to try harder. I recall an instance when one of my classmates who was a member of the football team attempted to tackle another player who weighed probably 50 or 60 pounds more that he. This unwise act resulted in the smaller player having been knocked pretty nearly into slumber land, but the coach's reaction to this scenario was that the smaller player had to try harder. These and hundreds of similar experiences helped me to establish the belief that if I failed at anything, it was a function of my not having tried hard enough.

Then there was the "work hard" driver. My first male role model was my father, a man who demonstrated by word and deed that hard work was redemptive. To my knowledge, he never missed a day from work during his productive years. When he would come home from work, he always found something to do around the yard or he would take me with him to a neighbor's house where he would perform charitable service for literally anyone who asked him. There were always plenty of odd jobs to be done at our house, and my father seemed to assume that it was a reflection of one's character to not find something that needed to be done. Hence I developed the concept that work was noble and that to not work was less than noble. Together with the two aforementioned concepts, I began to develop the pattern of hyperactivity that continues to follow me even until the present time. I have neither the ability for nor a level of tolerance of doing absolutely nothing, even though my intellect tells me that reasonable people take time away. I abhor the thought of being on an extended vacation where I have no avenue through which to fulfill my drive to work at something.

The driver over which I have experienced the greatest sense of recovery is the "hurry up" message that was so much a part of my development. When I was in the first grade, the students would always engage in competition to see who could complete our assignments quickest. Each of us wanted the prestige that came from walking up to the teacher's desk and handing in our work while the other poor devils were still struggling to finish theirs. When we were given our required standardized tests which always seemed to me to be only moderately challenging, the reward for finishing early was that one could go outside and play while the rest of the "slower" students agonized over the test. When given a task at home, I could anticipate that the directive to hurry up was forthcoming. The result of these and other such experiences helped me to develop the attitude that faster is superior to slower. Sometimes even now, when driving along an unfamiliar highway and discovering that I am lost, I am inclined to think that the solution is to drive faster. To follow this urge generally results in my getting farther from my intended destination.

The final driver that I will discuss here is the "please me" message. During my childhood, adults did not see a need to explain themselves to children. Being the inquisitive child that I was, I frequently asked the adults around me "why", and the answer was always the same reply, "because I said so". Case closed. Whenever we were assigned tasks of any kind, it seemed that these tasks were deemed to be completed well only when someone else had expressed their satisfaction with our effort. Even on my odd jobs for which I hired out, there was never pre-definition of the work to be done. I served at the pleasure of the boss. My job as I saw it was to please that person.

The reason for my relating these five sets of experiences is that of setting forth the premise that if we continue into adult life being influenced only by our childhood experiences, we miss the opportunity to grow from them. It is equally unwise to completely ignore these experiences for in them we can find some understanding of ourselves. The great danger of the influence of drivers such as these mentioned here is that at some point one realizes that they are receiving flawed messages from them. A negative reaction to this realization can be detrimental to the development of proper, effective responses and can translate into harmful behavior. For instance, at some point, one comes to realize that try as you may, you are not going to reach perfection. This realization can lead to rationalizing that it is useless to put forth a good effort when it is certain to end in a less than desirable outcome. A more beneficial response would be that of establishing a reasonable goal and the acceptance that progress toward that goal is a valid indicator of success. To measure one's self against the ideal of perfection is to guarantee that one will experience feelings of inadequacy. Feelings of success are a much greater motivator than are feelings of failure.

Trying harder does not necessarily lead to greater success. Most often, success is a result of gradual improvement. The old adage that practice makes perfect can be misleading. The truth is that practice makes permanent. If you are practicing without proper application of technique, you may be developing permanent habits that do not lead to success. An example of this is the would-be basketball player who is a playground hero but who has developed habits that hinder his ability to play under guidance from a college or professional coach. Another is the musically inclined person who has learned to play by ear through years of practice, but simply cannot comprehend formal instruction in music.

Trying harder is at best second to trying smarter. The latter involves taking note of the task before you and developing a logical approach to reaching your goal. For me, this would include consultation with others who have reached the goal toward which I am aspiring. It would include a sincere effort to eliminate the distractions that may inhibit my progress. And it would then include giving my best effort consistently. To the casual observer, I would indeed appear to be trying harder.

Working hard may be the greatest road block to success if that practice is not coupled with careful planning. Persons who rely on their perceived ability to overpower obstacles by the force of their effort are less likely to plan their course of action. When effective planning precedes action, less work is required to reach your goal. By working smarter, you will lessen the need to work as hard.

Hurrying up confuses speed with effectiveness. The meticulous person rarely hurries. The preparation of a gourmet meal requires much more time than the making of a spam sandwich. It is wise to be on task and to proceed with dispatch, but it is wiser to be deliberate in your undertakings. Once an action has been taken, that action cannot be recalled. Of course, you may take subsequent actions in an effort to offset the impact of a hasty action, but it is wiser to evaluate the likely consequence of an action before taking that action. The old adage "haste makes waste" certainly contains a powerful truth.

The "please me" driver has the potential to undercut one's self esteem. At some point, we will realize that many people operate from very selfish motives. They may even invoke the "I will love you if you…" message. We should realize that love is not conditional upon our pleasing someone, particularly someone who is seeking self-gratification at our expense. If we set as our goal that of behaving well toward others and of treating every person with respect, we will be less concerned with whether we please someone. We will become more concerned with inspecting our own behavior and how it may be improved to our own standard than to an artificial standard set by a self-appointed judge of our character.

Chapter IV

MEETING YOURSELF HALFWAY

A REASONABLE QUESTION TO ASK IS "is it possible to receive too much love?" Every now and then, we read stories about someone that loved someone so much that they resorted to murdering them because they could not bear the thought of their being with someone else. Is killing an act of love? Even more common is the act of spousal abuse or physical attack on a "loved one" by a partner who allegedly was driven by love to commit such acts.

The answer in each of the cited cases is that love must be defined in more positive terms to meet my standard. If you have set no standard, then you will have no response to behavior that is represented as acts of love when actually they are merely acts of power driven by the desire to control.

Most of us will not in our lives experience overt exploitation in the guise of love. However, we are more likely to present ourselves as victims being driven by our own desires to please the people in our lives. In so doing, we permit these self-imposed demands to rise to a level that greatly reduces the quality of life. The standard justification that we give for filling our lives with issues that are truly not our own is "she/he loves me, and I love him/her".

My personal awareness with the reality of the possibility of being loved to death began when I had reached the absolute summit of my professional career. I had just been named Associate State Superintendent for the North Carolina Department of Public Instruction which was at that time the highest non-elected position in the Department. I was sure that I was loved by every citizen of my state, and I wanted very much to please all of them. I wanted more than anything else to justify the decision that my supervisor had made in naming me to this position. I felt that in order to do these things, I would have to work hard, try harder, please everyone, hurry up, and be perfect. This I knew that I could do because I had always been driven by these directives, so off I went with that as my goal.

My first rude awakening was to the fact that there were not enough hours in a day in which to execute all the tasks that I had defined for myself. This realization led to my taking a seminar in time management. In this seminar, one point made stood out from all the rest…working late is a bad practice, because you are unproductive after a certain point. Instead, come in early and get a lot of work done before the activities of the day begin. I said to myself, "self, try that starting next Monday morning."

On the following Monday morning, I arrived at the office at 7:00 am. Since the office does not open officially until 8:00 am, I feel pretty certain that I have one full hour in which to catch up on my work that has piled up on my desk. Instead, as soon as I take my seat, the telephone rings. I wonder who would be calling my office one hour before it is scheduled to open for the day. Upon picking up the receiver, I hear a familiar voice saying, "Dud, are you busy right now?" I ask myself why I would be in the office one hour early were I not busy, but recognizing the voice as being that of my boss, I answer, "no, Craig, is there something that I can do for you?" Craig, my boss responds, "Can you come down to my office for a minute?" Now that may sound like a question. But be assured that when your boss asks in that manner, it is not a question. It is a coded message that really means, "Get in here right away". Unless you are involved in brain surgery, you are to drop whatever you were doing and be prepared to hear of something that is critical to the organization.

I go down to Craig's office and he assures me that this will take only a minute. Some thirty minutes later, I emerge from his office with some new work under my arm. Is this my work? Yes, now it is. Before I entered his office, that was his work, but now, not only is it mine, but it goes to the front of the line of things that must get done right away. But I am not disturbed by this, because Craig loves me, and I love him.

I arrive back at my office at 7:30, relieved that I still have half an hour before the work day officially begins. But before I can take my seat, I look up to see Gene Causby entering my office. Gene asks" hey, fellow, you got a minute?" On its face, this sounds like a question. Be assured that if your best friend is asking, it is a coded message that really means that you must decide whether what you are doing is more important to you than our friendship. The obvious answer is, "surely, I have a minute. Come on in and have a seat". Gene comes in and makes himself comfortable for the next twenty five minutes. I enjoy his company as I always do, but now the hour that I was saving has gone by the wayside. But Gene loves me, and I love Gene.

The time is now 7:55 am. I can finally get on with the work that I have arrived an hour early to do, or so I think. But today Shelia, my administrative assistant has decided to arrive early so that she can talk to me before the workday begins. As soon as Gene leaves, in she comes bringing with her a stack of telephone messages that appear to be about two or three inches thick. Each one of them is marked "URGENT". I ask

Shelia if any of the messages are more urgent than the rest. She points to one from a lady who has called three times and who has lost her patience with the agency at not having had the response that she is seeking.

Following a few minutes of briefing from Shelia, I dial the number for the disgruntled caller. When she answers the phone, I say to her, "Good morning, Mrs. Jones. I am Dudley Flood. I work in the office of the State Superintendent, and I understand that you have a concern that you want to share with me". In her most demanding voice, she responds, "It's about time somebody in authority called me. It has been two days since I called up there. What in the world do you folks do up there except sit around and drink coffee?" I respond, "Mrs. Jones, I am calling to see if I can be of some service to you with your concern". She continues, "How many folks work in that big building anyway?" I think to myself, "about half of them", but I respond to her again, "Mrs. Jones, is there something that I can do for you?" Mrs. Jones continues, "Do you realize that I am a citizen and a tax payer?" I think to myself, "does she think that I am an alien and a free-loader?", but I respond to her, "Mrs. Jones, my only reason for being here is to help you find a solution to your concern. How may I help you?" Having failed to get my goat, she begins to modify her voice tone. "You seem like a fairly nice young man, and I am sure that it is not your fault that the school bus did not pick up my child. Still, I would appreciate it if you would straighten out these people down here. They don't care anything about our children".

At last I know what the problem is. The bus did not come for her child on the first day of school. I asked, "Mrs. Jones, Have you spoken to the bus driver?" Mrs. Jones responded, "No, I didn't want to go that high up". I think to myself, this is some pretty good logic. The bus driver is local, so you call the State Superintendent's office rather that to talk to him. Still, I get right on the problem and within half an hour we have a solution for her. I call her back to report that the problem is solved and that a bus will be coming by her house in the very near future. Mrs. Jones says to me, "Mr. Flood, I just love you". I respond, "Mrs. Jones, I love you too." Truth be known, this love is getting pretty deep right about now.

As I return to the pile of telephone messages, I find one from my brother, James, which says call home when you get a break. I think to myself that this has to be important because James is a man of few words who calls only when it is critical to do so. I dial his number at the school at which he teaches and ask the secretary if he is in position to come to the phone. Knowing that this must be an emergency, she quickly gets him to the phone. James gets right to the point. "What have you got planned for this weekend?" he asks. I did have some plans that I was certain that he would not be interested in hearing about. I had managed to acquire two tickets to see Duke play UNC-Chapel Hill, each being ranked among the top ten basketball teams in the nation at the time. I had traded in two of the neighborhood's children to get those tickets.

Realizing that James did not really call to see what I had planned, I responded, "Not too much, what's up on your end?" "I thought you might like to see Elizabeth City State play Norfolk State this weekend", James responded. He already had the tickets, so I was pretty sure that this was not a question. After all, James attended Elizabeth City State and he still lives in northeastern North Carolina where the game between these two schools is an institution third to motherhood and Christianity. So my reply is "what time is the game?" Fortunately, I was able to trade my two tickets for an acre of land near Benson. I did not need to think long about my answer, because my brother loves me and I love my brother.

Shelia raps gently on my office door and announces that my wife is on the phone. Barbara never calls my office during the work day unless it is crucial to do so, so Shelia knows that I should take this call at once. Barbara has called to say that she has been thinking that I should take some time off so that we can spend it together away from the demands of our respective jobs. I know instinctively that she is absolutely right. We have not had a real vacation in recent memory. More importantly, she is only asking the same thing that everyone else is asking; that I make it clear that she is the most important person in my life.

I recognize that Craig is my boss, but he and Barbara are not required to have a positive relationship. Thankfully, they get alone well, but the biggest thing that they have in common is me. Gene and Barbara get alone fabulously, but in the end of it all, Gene is my friend and his relationship with Barbara is by happenstance. James is Barbara's very favorite family member, but she had wanted to see Duke and Carolina play each other. In the end, I am in the middle of a set of competing forces, all of which are expecting to be the most important thing in the world to me but which are not required to respond to the other forces. So I assure Barbara that we will take a vacation within the month, because Barbara loves me and I love her.

When you add the several forces that I have not mentioned here that are requiring a response from you but that are not related to each other, you are headed toward a stressful set of experiences. I am particularly sympathetic to people who have children, especially so to women. They seem to be most driven to win and maintain the love of their children at all costs. Barbara and I did not have children of our own although we have offered parenting to any number of children who seemed as close to us as they would have been had we been their biological parents. However, we did have another "family member" in the person of Barbara's dog, Prince. There is a whole story about how Prince joined our family.

This story is best understood in light of the fact that as head of the house, I make all the big decisions and Barbara makes all the little decisions. I decide things like whether America has a sound foreign policy or where the new civic center should be built. Barbara decides little things like where we shop, where we attend church and when we buy a new car or which doctor we use for our primary health care. To keep it simple, I have only two rules by which I govern our house; the first being that I do not try to run her life, and I do not try to run MY life. The second rule led to our acquiring a dog.

My second rule is that I do not waste money on myself. If I spend any non-critical money, I always spend it on my wife. Following this practice, I had bought Barbara a four wheel drive Chevrolet pick up truck. I had bought the truck so that she would be able to pull the boat that I had previously bought for her. On an occasion when I was driving Barbara's truck, pulling her boat down to the coast, we saw a couple in a truck just like hers that had a shot gun rack over the rear window and a cage on the back that held a beautiful beagle hound. I knew immediately that we were missing something, so I went right out and bought Barbara a twelve gage shot gun. I suggested to her that she might need a dog so that we could better fit into our new culture. That is when things started to go down hill. Barbara announced to me that she and her mother had spoken to a friend about a dog that she would soon be acquiring.

As it turned out, the dog in question was a mixed blood, half collie and half German shepherd. This breed has long hair that sheds freely, and the notion of having a dog sleep in our house required some adjustment for me. My concept of dogs was that they were outdoor pets. Further, Barbara named the dog Prince, which in my mind established a pecking order since my name is not King. The dog grew like wildfire. By the time it was six months old, it stood taller than I when on its hind legs, which it frequently was.

On a typical day, I would work until possibly nine of ten at night. Upon my returning home, I could expect Prince, who had spent most of the day lying across our air conditioner vents, running up our fuel bill, to meet me at the door, rise up on his hunches to lick my face and then to lock himself around my leg and rub vigorously. Having had enough of this kind of attention, I might say to him, "Prince! Sit!" upon which Barbara was sure to respond, "don't speak to him like that, he is doing that because he loves you". I am thinking to myself, "He is doing that because that feels good to the dog. This has nothing to do with me". Then I reflect on the fact that even the dog is in this way like everyone that I have encountered; he wants to be the most important thing in my life, and he wants it right now.

There is a solution to this state of affairs by which everyone wins. It has worked for me for years and I believe that it can work for others. First, I recognize that I can do only one thing well at a time. Therefore, I have resolved to always give due diligence to whatever I am doing and to not allow my effort to be diminished by external distractions. That way, everything that I do has first priority in its turn. If I permit distractions to intervene, I will do less well and no one will feel that they have been given preferential treatment. Most people are willing to wait their turn if the result is that they will have quality attention given to their respective issue.

Secondly, I begin each day by asking myself a series of personal questions and by answering them as honestly as I can. Then I act on those answers as I go about my daily affairs. The first question that I raise with myself is "do you still enjoy that which you have selected as your life's work?" When I first began the practice of asking myself this question, I frequently found myself hedging on the answer. I might answer "most of the time, I do" or "after all, I do have a job" or something less than a direct answer based on a full assessment of my daily activities. However, after some practice and some thought, I learned to evaluate my activities differently. To my surprise, I discovered that about 85% of what I do, I like it well enough that I would do it free of charge if I could afford to, and about 15% of what I do sucks. Then I resolved to not wallow in the fifteen percent, but rather to glory in the eighty-five percent and to try to move more things into that category. Today, I am probably at 90% satisfaction, and I accept the other 10% as things that simply go with the territory that I occupy.

The next question that I ask myself is "do you worry selectively?" Indiscriminant worry can be detrimental to the making of progress and rarely leads to a solution of any of life's problems. You may use energy in worrying that might have been better spent in searching for solutions. My advice is to do whatever is within your power to improve a situation but to recognize the degree to which you have control over a given matter and do not charge yourself with matters that are beyond your span of influence. There are enough places in which you can make a difference that you will seldom find yourself idle, and the idle mind is most prone to unhealthy worry.

Then I ask myself "from whom do you seek affirmation and validation?" Many people that I have met seem to have the need for someone else to approve of their thoughts and values before they are able to act on them. There are instances in which advice is useful, but it is unlikely that others can fully understand your specific perspective because it is based on so many of your personal experiences that you have shared with no one. Generally, advice begins with the observation, "if I were you, I would..." which may or may not be true since the advisor is not you nor does he or she know what it is like to be you. A more helpful statement may have acknowledged that "from what I understand about the situation you are facing, my best advice to you is"... This leaves open the fact that the decision is still yours and that you may act on my advice if you find it to be useful. If not, you must continue to look within yourself for the strategy that you can apply.

My next question to myself is "what kinds of excuses do you give yourself for failing to do something about an undesirable condition in your life?" Some years ago, I was in conversation with a gentleman who was an unsuccessful school teacher and who had expressed to me his dislike for the profession. I asked him if there were not something else that he might find more satisfying as a profession, to which he responded that he had always wanted to practice law. My advice to him was to consider applying to a law school and to move toward the accomplishment of his dream. His response to me was that he was now too old to follow that dream. "I am thirty years old" he said. "Do you realize how old I would be by the time I finished law school?" I replied that it takes most people about three years to complete the required work for that profession. Then I asked him "how old are you going to be in three years if you do not go to law school?" Could it be that you are asking yourself the wrong question? You are going to be thirty-three either way. The real issue is whether you are willing to make the same effort that is required of everyone else who has become an attorney or if you are satisfied with the excuse that you are too old to accept that challenge. Our great danger is not that we so often fail in our quest for success, but that we so readily accept excuses for not applying our abilities toward that end.

I conclude my self- interrogation by asking, "are you prepared to deal with adversity?" Most of us do well when things are going well for us. However, when adversity strikes, many of us seem to lose focus on our strengths and begin to react emotionally rather than rationally. This is the very time that we need most to employ our mental and psychological attributes.

The old saying, "prepare for war in the time of peace" has application to dealing with adversity. When you are intellectually and psychologically prepared for a challenge, it is less likely that you will be overcome by it. Indeed, you may even begin to look forward to the occasion to apply your problem solving skills.

When we were young, my brother and I were given to going snake hunting on occasion. Knowing the adversarial nature on such an activity caused us to prepare in advance to deal successfully with the matter at hand. We went to great lengths to study the nature and habits of snakes. Among other things, we learned that a snake is most lethargic right after it has had a meal, so we observed to see if one had eaten before we approached it. Since snakes do not chew their food, we could see the imprint of small prey that it had swallowed in its stomach. This snake would be easier to take than would a lean and hungry one. We further observed that when lifting a captured snake to put it in our carrying cage, it was best to do so with the application of the least amount of force possible because force invites resistance.

There were several other lessons to be learned from our snake hunting experience such as the value of team work, having proper respect for the adversary, and using good judgment as to which challenge in which to engage. Most of all, we learned that proper preparation for a task reduces the danger of failing at that task, and that experience can be a very good teacher. The more often we did it the right way, the better we became at that task. Today, being fifty years removed from that activity, I would be very unsuccessful at that art. I now lack the psychological element to prepare properly and the physical dexterity to act appropriately rather than react, so I have conceded that for me to engage in such an activity would be unwise.

In answering these questions for myself, I remind myself that most of my success is in my hands. While there are other factors that make that final determination, these mentioned herein seem to be a very sound starting point toward success and happiness.

Chapter V

Different Does Not Mean Deficient

I BEGAN MY TEACHING CAREER AT a time when students were being grouped in classes according to their perceived ability. Each student was tested and was placed into a class made up of students whose test scores were similar. They were referred to as divisions and assigned a number in the order of their expected level of performance. Division one would be the more advanced students and so on.

In one of my classes, I had division four students. The norm in this class was in the lower one/forth of the class as a whole. A few weeks after the opening of school, we received a transfer student whose academic file had not yet reached us, so the principal placed him in that class to be served until his file arrived. When his file finally arrived, we learned that he was in the upper ten percent of the total class, but while he was in the lower group, the other students constantly complained that there was something wrong with him. The reason was that he was different and was therefore thought to be deficient.

Throughout my years of working with the issues surrounding school desegregation, I found a consistent pattern of thinking that had its origin in the discomfort that many of us find when dealing with people who are different from us. On its face, it may be thought of as a bias, but a deeper investigation may lead to the conclusion that it is more of a fear of the unfamiliar that prompts us to respond negatively to difference. The manifestation of this way of thinking can be found in the manner that we form our relationships with others.

Since we tend to be more comfortable with others who share common qualities, values, and characteristics, it followers logically that we group ourselves into monolithic groups to the degree that we can. These groups are formed around virtually any definable indicator that suggests sameness. Having grouped ourselves in this manner, we proceed to inculcate the qualities, values, beliefs, folkways and mores that we determine to be peculiar to our particular group. In so doing, we are able to pass our culture from one generation to the next.

One predicable result of this societal configuration is that in passing on our ways of life to our young, we may inadvertently fail to validate other cultures that are different from ours. The absence of such validation can lead to the thinking that if others are not just like we, there is something wrong with them. Hence, difference begins to be seen as deficiency.

Among the divisions into which we find ourselves are those of geographical location, political philosophy, religion, economic status, gender, age and race. There are many others, but these are so readily observable that they tend to rise to the top of the list of ways in which we separate ourselves from others.

Our normal process of passing on our cultural traits to others is that of ranking our choices in a superior posture as compared to those whose are different from ours. In so doing, we tend to project the choices of others in a negative light, not selectively, but in a blanket fashion. A commonly heard phrase that is used to categorize others is "you know how THEY are". Some go on to add "you see one, you've seen them all". An extension of this practice results in our assigning characteristics to others indiscriminately without knowing very much about a given individual. He or she begins to be regarded as a part of a mass that we have defined negatively. In so doing, we are relieved of the responsibility to respect each individual and to attribute merit where merit is due.

The history of the development of our nation lends itself to certain divisions among us, notably among which is our geography. Dating back to the great Civil War, we have attached some connotations to the essence of living in the North vs. living in the South. Many of us have formed a definition of ourselves and others around this one factor. My own experience has highlighted this practice As I travel the country, I have come to expect to encounter people who have never been to my home state and who know no one on a personal level who is from there, but who have some very rigid perceptions of what the people there are like, how they think, speak and behave.

A few years ago, I was invited to speak to a gathering of educators at a national conference held in the upper New York area. After having spoken for some forty five minutes, I mingled with the conferees to continue our discussion informally. One very gracious person approached me with the question that I have learned to expect, "where did you say that you are from?" I responded, "I am from North Carolina." The questioner asked, "Have you lived there all your life?" I responded, "Not yet". After we had enjoyed a good laugh, I asked her why she had asked about where I had lived and for how long. She explained to me that I did not sound like a North Carolinian. However, in further discussion, I learned that I was the first North Carolinian with whom she had spoken directly.

This is not a one sided issue. Those of us who live in the South have formed some inaccurate generalizations about those who live in the North, and are equally likely to act upon those beliefs.

Another of the divisions into which we tend to gravitate is that of rural versus urban. It appears that persons who were nurtured in an urban setting tend to have a negative predisposition toward persons who are from a rural setting. The same tends to be true of those from rural experiences having a negative view of these from the "inner city". Each group is influenced by stereotypic traits having been assigned to these respective groups as though ever person in either of the groupings meets these specifications.

When I was in undergraduate school, there were a sizable number of students from rural areas who would not acknowledge their home town because it was such a certainty that one would be labeled according to where he or she was from. People who were from the South and especially the rural South were assumed to be less sophisticated and generally less well prepared than those from major population centers. The facts did not bear this out. But that seemed not to lessen that perception. On the other hand, we who were from those rural areas tended to think of the city folks as thugs, hoodlums, renegades and brigands. Neither was this assumption borne out by the facts, but they served in categorizing those about which you knew little or nothing.

Economic position has always served as an indication of the status to which society assigns individuals. This assignment is more direct than some others in that we spell out status relations through it. If we have money, we are regarded as "upper class"; if we do not have money we are called "lower class"; and if society does not know whether we have money, we are called "middle class". The description of upper class people may best be obtained from lower class people who will assure you that these are ruthless folk who will cheat, usurp, victimize and take advantage of others. "If you see one, you have seen them all". Upper class people can best depict lower class people. They are lazy, shiftless, and under-motivated; all they want are handouts. If you see one, you've seen them all."

It should be noted that in every case of assigned characteristics, the attributed qualities are unflattering. This practice persists wherever a monolithic group defines a group about which they know little. Its origin is found in the desire to inculcate our own ideals even to the exclusion of all others, leading to the inevitable conclusion that different is undesirable because it is inferior to our way.

In matters of race, there is a sense of heightened urgency to proclaim difference as being a deficiency because in our society there appears to be a psychopathological preoccupation with race to the degree that we tend to see every human interaction in a racial context. For some of us there seems to be a hyper-vigilance to examine the racial implications of even the most mundane human interaction. In doing so, we tend to inject racial implications where none exist.

One may wonder how we came to a point where differences seem to be so very threatening to us. I shall cite two personal experiences that may shed some light on how we acquired some of our attitudes.

As a child, I lived in the town of Winton in North Carolina, a town of fewer that 500 people. In that town was one combination drug store and soda fountain. Each day after school, those of us who had a nickel would stop by Craig's Drug Store and order a cone of ice cream. We never had to specify the flavor because all they had was vanilla. After having engaged in this practice for several years, I was convinced that the best ice cream in the world was vanilla.

When I became a teenager, I was permitted to go to Atlantic City, New Jersey during the summers where I found employment in Fralinger's Ice Cream Parlor. There we had more than fifteen flavors of ice cream. I nearly went berserk sampling the various offerings. Upon my return home at the end of the summer, I could hardly contain myself until I could get to Craig's Drug Store to request of the management that they begin to carry some chocolate, coffee, strawberry, black walnut and peach ice cream. I was told in no uncertain terms "kid, if you are going to live here, you had better learn to like vanilla."

This was my first recognition of the fact that in certain societies, your venturing into areas not peculiar to that society is not readily welcomed. Your efforts to infuse your new knowledge gained through such ventures may be met with rejection. You will have to be particularly strong in your conviction to prevail against tradition and popular sentiment.

My second learning experience grew out of the tradition that if you were a child growing up in Winton, one of your great thrills was to go over to the neighboring town of Ahoskie on Saturday. You did not have to have a reason to go, but you knew that it would be only on Saturday that your parents would take you there. My brother and I would go to stand around and watch the A & P truck being unloaded, the most exciting thing that we were going to see that day.

One day, our parents told us to get ready to go to Ahoskie, but we noted that it was on Wednesday, so we inquired as to what could possibly be important enough for us to go during the middle of the week. Our father explained that today would be our only opportunity to see something that we had never seen before. He said, "Today, you are going to see a Republican". Now that struck a cord with me, for having never seen a Republican but having heard about them for as long as I could remember, I could barely contain myself. I "knew how they were". I had heard from the people that I most well trusted and respected, all of whom were Democrats, how Republicans were. I cannot recall having ever heard a single redeeming feature accorded to them.

A prevailing portrayal was that a former Republican candidate for office had promised that "If I am elected, there will be chicken on the table and two cars in every garage". I had noted that we did not get our two cars, but I reasoned that perhaps it was because we did not have a garage. In any case, we arrived at the destination on Railroad Street where we saw a train flat car decorated in red, white and blue. This was to be the stage from which the Republican would speak. Finally, several men came out and occupied the chairs on the stage. I finally, asked, "Dad, when are they going to bring out that Republican"? He answered, "The gentleman in the third chair to the left is he". I was virtually in shock. Here was an ordinary man, no horns, no tail. My father asked "What were you expecting to see"? I did not answer, because I knew that he did not realize what the negative comments that I had heard all my life had led me to think. I truly expected to see someone who was very different from the people around whom I had lived. I was certain that since he was different, he would in some ways be deficient.

What, then, might we do to begin to re-write the scripts that have such a great potential to obscure our true perception of other humans. For me, five directives have been extremely helpful to that end.

First, learn all that you can learn about people who are different from you; whether they are different by race, gender, age, economic condition, political preference, ethnicity, or in any other way. Draw no conclusion about any person or group of persons until you shall have learned about them in great depth.

Secondly, when you shall have sufficiently learned, compare what you have learned to what you had previously thought. In doing so, you are able to weigh the viability of your new information against that to which you may have been exposed for years and years.

My experience that brought light to this necessity grew out of the fact that in my having been reared in eastern North Carolina, I had developed some perceptions about people who were reared elsewhere in the state. Although I grew up in a home in which prejudice was greatly discouraged, I was convinced that the best people in the world were those from eastern North Carolina. The logical conclusion therefore was that those from elsewhere were not as good as we. I was leery of those from the Piedmont and was absolutely certain that those mountaineers were to be avoided. I have read comic books about L'il Abner, the Kentucky "hillbilly" and about Barney Google and Snuffy Smith, the West Virginia happy-go-lucky "good ole boys", and I found nothing with which I could identify in either.

Several years into my professional career, I met a young white man whose name was Gene Causby. By this time, I was residing in Greenville, North Carolina, still a good eastern town, and Gene was residing in Goldsboro, North Carolina, also a good eastern town. Gene and I eventually found ourselves teaming to work as the North Carolina Department of Public Instruction's technical assistance team charged with assisting with the desegregation of the state's public schools. In that role, we were together more frequently than we were with our respective families, and we became the very best of friends. As far as I was concerned, we had everything imaginable in common. We had each been school principals, had each been athletic coaches, each were lovers of music, and each enjoyed good clean humor. We were never bored with the company of each other.

On one of our many trips around the state to work with school districts, we found ourselves in the mountains of North Carolina as nightfall was nearing. I reminded Gene that we were a five hour drive from Raleigh where we now made our homes and that we had better head on down the mountain. To my great surprise, Gene responded that we should just spend the night in the area and drive home the following day. When I offered the excuse that we would likely not be able to find a hotel room for the night, he countered with the idea that we could spend the night with his parents. Now I had all along assumed that his parent were in Goldsboro, a good eastern town where I had assumed that he had grown up. He shared with me that he had grown up in Morganton and that his parents would be happy to have us stay with them. This for me was the moment of soul searching. My first thought was here is a "Hill Billy" sitting right on my front seat, and he has been "passing" for eastern all these years. What am I to believe, that which I had thought, taught and lived for thirty years, or that which I had learned from five years of practically living with a wonderful human being? Thankfully, I chose to accept my own experience as the viable basis on which to make my decision. The results of that decision can be seen by anyone who has been in the presence of Gene and me over the past 39 years. We continue to live our conviction, not for show, but because we both are grateful for how much richer our lives have been made by our relationship.

The third charge for changing our attitude and behavior is to resolve to act on our new information. I have always thought that if we knew better, we would do better. Still, I have worked with people who I am certain learned the flaw in their previous thinking but who persisted in that train of thought notwithstanding their knowledge to the contrary. A personal commitment is necessary for one to vary from a course of comfort and to challenge old folkways and mores that have been a way of life for many years.

Fourth, we must begin to create ways and attitudes that lead to positive human relationships. There is no one set of strategies that will work well for everyone. Each of us must find his or her comfort zone in dealing with others. Just remember that practice makes permanent. If we begin to practice respect for others and to seek to better understand people who are not like we, it soon becomes a way of life and no longer will require a conscious effort on our part.

Finally, we must resolve to never generalize that any group of people can be defined by one set of qualities. We are individuals and deserve to be regarded as such. The one feature that we all share in common is that we belong to the human race, and that entitles us to the right to be respected.

History reminds us that we have always had more in common than is reflected in our differences. History reports that during the westward expansion in our nation's youth, there was for a time ongoing hostility between the Native Americans, then called American Indians, and the soldiers charged to protect the settlers. At the close of these hostilities, the Shoshone Chief Yellow Hand was invited to deliver remarks at the signing of the peace treaty. On the occasion, Chief Yellow Hand, who was not fond of oratory, said simply these words: "There are many kinds of birds; red birds, blue birds, white birds, black birds; all birds. There are many kinds of horses; brown horses, bay horses, paint horses, gray horses; all horses. There are many kinds of men; white men, red men, brown men, yellow men, black men; all men."

If we truly believe that all men and women are just that, men and women, then we can accept that different does not mean deficient.

Chapter VI

THE UNFINISHED BUSINESS OF SCHOOL DESEGREGATION

THE LANDMARK DECISION RENDERED IN the case known as Brown vs. Board of Education opened the door for progress throughout American society. I have seen progress that I had never expected to see within my lifetime. However, there remains a tremendous amount of unfinished business to reach the full promise of equal educational opportunity for all.

The pressing issue of school desegregation in its early stages was that of providing equal access to educational opportunity for all students. This process consisted mainly of the removal of legal barriers which denied certain groups access to schooling. The unfinished business of school desegregation is that of providing equal access to <u>success</u> in this society for all its members. Having education does not provide a guarantee of success, nor should it, but it does greatly improve the likelihood of one's success. Therefore, the burden and challenge which schools now face is that of ensuring that all children have equal access to <u>knowledge</u> which leads to success in our society.

Staffing patterns in schools still tend to reflect the vestiges of segregation. Some school systems in America employ no Black professional personnel. In an even greater number of systems, all the decision-making positions within the central administration are occupied by Whites. Such staffing patterns tend to reinforce the myth that Blacks are incapable of functioning in decision-making roles. The concomitant negative effect is that Blacks cannot realistically aspire to occupy these positions and feel it a waste of their energy to prepare themselves academically to hold these positions. Therefore, the absence of "qualified Blacks" is also self-perpetuating.

Although the concern over discipline problems in America's public schools appears to have decreased in recent years, minority students are still much more likely to be cited for misbehavior at school than are White students. This fact may be due, in part, to the fact that the behavior patterns that are rewarded in school are those behaviors indigenous to White culture, thereby giving an additional educational advantage to children who were nurtured within that culture.

Some improvement has occurred in the area of curriculum development in recent years, but there is still evidence of under-inclusion of the contributions of Blacks and other minorities. Such under-inclusion strengthens the myth that these groups have made no meaningful contributions to this society.

As education moves forward toward the completion of the unfinished business of desegregation, educators must examine the illusions of improvement. We must re-dedicate and re-sensitize ourselves to work to avoid tracking schemes, lack of balance in curricula, lower expectations of minority students to achieve and other such practices which have a negative impact on students to achieve.

Schools must foster an atmosphere in which no child is socialized to achieve at a level less than his or her ability. Since public school is the only institution which accommodates children from all segments of our society, it must provide the practice field upon which Americans can learn and implement equal status relationships. Only when these steps have been taken will America reach the full potential of progress that was made possible by the Brown decision.

Since the Brown decision of 1954, many of those responsible for administering education have been seriously engaged in the process of dismantling and removing the vestiges of the dual school concept and moving to a unitary school concept. While so doing, they have carried the continued responsibility for maintaining the highest standards of education possible for all the student population.

Over the past 54 years, education has come through the various phases which have characterized most social change. First, that of open resistance from those whose vested interests seemed threatened, and of fear and anxiety by those upon whom the responsibility to initiate change rested most heavily. Secondly, having reluctantly resigned ourselves to the inevitability of change, and having determined how to achieve the least amount acceptable to our collective conscience in the least disruptive manner. Finally, to the point of having given new ideas a reasonable chance to work, and having come to the conclusion that both the school population and the nation's interest are better served when all citizens are afforded equal access to educational opportunities.

The Supreme Court ruled in 1955 that schools in the de jute school districts must make a "good faith start in the transformation from a dual to a unitary school system with all deliberate speed." To meet this mandate, many de jure districts adopted the concept of "freedom of choice."

Under the freedom of choice concept, school boards generally provided in their policies that any student may elect to attend any school within the district with transportation being provided at public expense.

Several features of freedom of choice gave it the appearance of a logical course of responsible action. One was the fact that having selected a school by choice, students frequently came with a greater incentive to do well in school. Moreover, parents seemed more prone to support the school to which their children were assigned in response to their choice. Often, their level of support was greater than it had been previously for the racially homogenous school. Many of the minority group students who transferred into previously white schools came from supportive homes. Having had multi-cultural experiences and parental support and guidance, these students generally adjusted well to their new surroundings. For them, freedom of choice appeared to be producing desirable results.

Freedom of choice, on the other hand, did grave damage to many of the racially homogenous minority schools. In some cases, the transferring of many of the higher level academic students away from these schools resulted in a lowering of the achievement norms of those schools. This frequently was accompanied by a reduction of community support for these schools and often resulted in a negative modification of their educational climate. Many top athletes, scholars, and student leaders left the Black and American Indian schools, taking with them school spirit, pride, and heritage. The schools which had served minorities exclusively began to lose their long-standing position as the center of community activities.

By the year 1973, many North Carolina school districts had adopted plans for complete desegregation and others were in the process of devising such plans. As desegregation became more and more a reality, new problems emerged and some old problems were brought into clearer focus. Some of the more visible problems facing educational leaders in North Carolina in the late sixties and early seventies were the following:

1. How to develop in-service training programs designed to help staff to make the transition from a dual to a unitary school with a minimum of anxiety and loss of effectiveness.

2. How to develop programs directed toward obtaining and strengthening community support for school desegregation.

3. How to develop administrative and instructional organizations designed to cope with the problems arising from desegregation.

4. How to coordinate all educational efforts where appropriate so as to bring all these efforts to bear on the problems of school desegregation.

5. How to respond to crisis situations related to school desegregation which may arise from time-to-time.

6. How to develop long-range and comprehensive programs and plans to solve problems incident to schools desegregation.

7. How to develop curricula offerings which would provide quality learning experiences for all students.

8. How to make maximum use of available services provided by other agencies outside the sphere of public education to assist with desegregation-related issues.

The degree to which these problems were overcome varied from district to district. An examination of the factors which operated in a particular district would be necessary in order that one might have a complete picture as to the reasons for progress, or the lack of progress experienced by that district. Generally, the following factors tended to determine the complexity of the problem for a specific district:

1. The demographic composition of the district and its political subdivisions.

2. How that district was affected by the actions of Federal court orders and/or Federal guidelines.

3. How community pressures had been exerted upon local school leadership.

4. The effects of historical separation of the races, not only in education but in many other areas of life and living within that particular community.

5. The tendency of organizations and people to "take sides" on issues.

6. Politics and the political climate within a particular school district.

7. Economics factors, such as cost of living, per capita income, tax base, etc.

These are merely examples of the factors which did affect the schools and in turn affected their ability to solve the problems of school desegregation.

The present trend in the nation is clearly toward complete and total desegregation of the public schools. While polls taken in the country consistently show that a great number of people oppose such concepts as busing to achieve racial balance, they also show that an overwhelming majority of Americans believe that no one should be discriminated against on the grounds of race, color, or national origin. It is upon this belief that the future of equal educational opportunity rests.

As educators look toward the future, we must recognize and plan ahead to deal with a new dimension of desegregation. Many of the old problems remain with us in modified versions. In addition, new problems emerge as a district progresses through the various phases of desegregation. Some of the more recent concerns are described briefly in the following paragraphs.

1. <u>Resegregation in Schools</u> – There persists a tendency toward maintaining group identity within the desegregated school. Students tend to isolate themselves racially at free periods and in the lunchroom. Some schools find that elective courses reflect an over inclusion of one race. Students tend to identify racially with certain subject areas and to pursue certain vocations, in spite of available guidance presumably acquainting students with the full scope of options available to them.

2. <u>Students' Attitudes</u> – There appears to be a sizeable portion of the student population which still fails to identify with the objectives of the concept of school desegregation, those objectives being to provide each student with the highest quality of education he or she is capable of consuming. Some students still harbor negative racial attitudes and beliefs which diminish their ability to work with students and teachers of a race different from their own. Others seem unwilling to involve themselves in competition with other races, whether such competition be academic, athletic or in displaying of other talents and skills.

3. <u>Teachers' Attitudes</u> - While many teachers have accepted the challenge to work for progress in school desegregation, there are still those among the ranks who either cannot or will not modify their stereotypical impressions of other races. This factor can drastically alter their effectiveness with a racially mixed class. Moreover, these teachers generally relate poorly to parents of a different race and sometimes to other professionals within the building.

4. <u>Attitudes of Schools Administrators</u> – The administrator of a desegregated school may find the leadership style with which he or she is most comfortable, and which was effective in previous situations, to

be completely ineffective in the desegregated school setting. For this principal to enjoy full success and effectiveness may necessitate additional training, additional sensitivity to those whose needs the school must serve and new approaches to address "routine" matters.

5. Community Involvement in the Schools – The established tradition of identifying with the neighborhood school greatly lessened when schools were desegregated. Too often, this was replaced by disdain for schools which "are no longer ours" in minds of community leaders of all races. New directions in educational planning must restore the opportunity and the belief in school involvement to those who are most directly affected.

6. Lack of Visibility of Minority Leadership – Historically, school desegregation has tended to result in a reduction of status and visibility of a disproportionate number of minority leaders. The absence of either the visibility or power of minority leaders fosters a larger number of minority youth who lack confidence in the value of education as a vehicle for personal advancement.

7. Curriculum Design – The tendency toward broad based curriculum design is being seriously threatened by the perceived pressure to teach to the standardized tests. It is clear to those experienced in curriculum development that even a broader based curriculum may be necessary to best meet the needs of a multi-cultural student population.

8. Appropriate Guidance for Minority Students – There is clearly a need for guidance to become a more individualized process in the desegregated schools. Those who counsel must have more than a superficial awareness of the community based problems facing minority youths, and of the influence outside of school which must be complemented, supplemented or offset as these students establish their life goals.

Desegregation of schools is not an end but is a means to an end. The desired outcome in that every citizen will be equipped to participate on an equal basis in the social, political, economic, educational and religious institutions which determine the quality of life which Americans enjoy. So long as access to these institutions is influenced by factors such as race, gender, age, national origin, economic class, religious preference or handicapping condition, desegregation is not achieving its intended objective. The public schools are the centerpiece of our society and they provide the only vehicle through which full opportunity for all citizens in our nation can be realized.

Our focus must be on building the future rather than on simply undoing the past. Our efforts can produce favorable results.

Chapter VII

THE CHALLENGE:
A POSITIVE FOCUS ON THE
AFRICAN AMERICAN MALE

A MAJOR CONCERN WITHIN THE BLACK community is that of the lack of success with schooling of the male child. This lack of success is reflected in higher unemployment, higher incarceration rates, higher crime and drug use rates and lower literacy rates found within this group than within the general population.

Such a pattern begins within the first five years of life for many children, and effective intervention must take place much earlier than is now the rule. One approach is to develop early intervention programs which target minority group males. This would begin with the development of opportunities for parents and interested persons to generate ideas and strategies for attacking this problem.

Most of us recognize that in addition to the family support we received during our formative years, we also experienced valuable nurturing from other basic institutions within our respective communities. Even the most remote areas of North Carolina provided growth experiences through faith establishments (churches), social clubs, Girl Scouts and Boy Scouts, 4-H Clubs, and other such programs. Many of today's youth have had little or no exposure to such experiences. Our population has grown beyond the capacity of our social organizations, leaving more of the nurturing responsibility to the biological parents. At the same time, the negative influences that might intervene in child development are at an all time high. These factors compel us to seek to create a shared strategy to address these shared problems.

In a free society, so much rides on one's having a sound education that it is immoral to not educate every child. Our society must join hands to establish a moral imperative in support of the idea of providing an effective, appropriate educational experience for all children.

While we acknowledge that there are no simple solutions to a matter as complex as the issue of effective education for all youth, there are some things that we have learned that may help us toward that objective. These learnings include the following considerations.

1. **Develop Programs Designed to Help Parents to Guide the Education of Their Children**

   There appears to be a high correlation between the success of a child in school and his or her parents' ability to direct the child's educational experiences. We need to develop programs designed to lead the parent toward decisions in the selection of curricula, building relationships with school personnel, helping with homework, and other such enhancing activities.

2. **Work to Maintain Minority Presence Within the Teaching and Educational Administration Work Force**

   Some school systems seem not to place a value on the hiring and retention of minority teachers and administrators. Communities must use their collective voices to amplify the needs of minority youth to have available to them living examples of capable, contributing members of their own race to help them to conceptualize their own capabilities and to develop their own self esteem. Further, communities must support efforts to recruit and maintain minority personnel within their school system.

3. **Create After School Programs to Improve Academic and Social Skills**

Many minority youth have no safe, supervised environment in which to spend their early evening and late afternoon hours. Communities must create after school programs designed to provide opportunities for supervised study, social development or wholesome recreation for children whose working parents may not be available to them until later in the evening.

4. **Faith Based Organizations Provide Appropriate Role Models for Minority Youth**

The historic notion of separation of church and state may have led to the perception that the two must maintain clear cut, separate identities and therefore may not engage cooperatively in joint activities. In truth, churches are a logical source of role models which by near common consent are sorely needed in the schools. The conspicuous presence of adults with whom students identify generally leads to improved student behavior and increased academic participation by those students.

5. **Establish Grade Mothers/Fathers**

The needs of some children may go undetected because there is not a strategy in place to discover such needs. Schools need to designate persons as grade parents. These persons would be assigned to a particular grade or class and would work with the teacher to monitor the progress of the children therein, gathering information to alert parents of problems which a particular child may experience. The community then uses its collective resources to generate appropriate solutions to these problems.

6. **Promote Sensitivity to the Needs of Minority Children**
   Along with the need for more minority teachers and administrators is the equally important need to have more educators who are sensitive to the peculiar needs of minority youth. The State Department of Pubic Instruction should design staff development programs to better equip educators to work more effectively with culturally diverse populations. Higher education institutions should also include such training in their teacher preparation programs.

7. **Create Opportunities for Minority Students to Develop Their Ability to Compete Successfully in Non-Class Activities**
   Minority children tend to be under-represented in non-athletic extra-class activities which lead to the development of their leadership abilities. Minority children could profit from exposure to such activities as public speaking, debating, conducting meetings, leadership training, and holding student offices.

8. **Promote the Use of Minority Personalities as Impact Educators**
   Many schools provide for their students the opportunity to hear citizens who have excelled in their respective fields. These persons may make a lasting impact on young people who are forming their own goals and identities. Schools should strive to expose all students to positive minority personalities who have achieved within their lifetimes.

9. **Provide Mentors for Minority Youth**
   Many successful adults attribute much of their development to their having had one or more mentors during their formative years who had a profound influence on their lives. Schools

need to engage mentors which pair minority youth with strong, positive personalities who can provide educational direction and incentive.

10. Establish SAT Study Courses

Minority students continue to score less well on the Scholastic Aptitude Test than do their majority race school mates. Public school systems should work with community colleges to establish programs designed to teach test-taking skills and to acquaint minority students with the format of tests such as the SAT.

What We Have Learned:

We need to look past "blame" in describing the problems that our youth face. Instead, we need to borrow on the collective recourses within our communities to generate new strategies for reaching those children who need our help. There is room in this quest for all who care about our future.

Chapter VIII

THE EFFECTIVE LEADER

A FEW YEARS AGO, MY PARTNER Gene Causby and I were involved in providing leadership training for principles in the public schools of North Carolina. The training sessions were held in various locations around the state, and some principals were sent against their preference to participate. On the printed program as a topic for the sessions were the words: If They Are Not Following, You Are Not Leading. One young administrator found this reference to be offensive. He approached the front of the room and in his firmest voice stated "I AM a leader, but the idiots won't follow".

Upon this note, we took the opportunity to share with him that a brief time prior to that occasion, we had spoken at a dog food convention called by a company that had been among the nations leaders in dog food sales, but had recently experienced a dramatic decline in sales. Prior to introducing us as speakers for the day, the CEO took the podium and began to prep the audience to be prepared to be motivated. He challenged the assembly by asking "Who has the best dog food in the nation?" to which they responded in unison, "We do". He continued, "Who has the best organization in this business?" They again responded

"We do". This was followed by several additional questions each of which received the same answer, "We do". Now the CEO looks a bit puzzled. He asks "Then why are we not selling any more dog food than we are?" One very animated individual popped up from his seat and shouted "The d--- dogs won't eat it."

The moral of the story is that if the dogs do not eat your dog food, do not look at the dogs but rather look at the dog food. In that same vein, if people are not following, don't look at the people but rather look at your leadership practices.

There are some clearly recognizable qualities and practices that are evident in effective leaders. Several of these will be discussed in this presentation. It must first be noted that we have not classified leaders as good or bad but rather as effective or ineffective. Effective leaders are able to get other people to do things that they may otherwise not have done. The most effective of these are the leaders who can cause people to want to do things that they otherwise may not have wanted to do. Such a leader is likely to have the following characteristics or to engage in the following activities.

MAKES TOUGH DECISIONS

Many people are fond of making minor decisions that will have little possibility of negative consequences, but shy away from making what could be career-altering decisions. When such major issues arise, they are prone to defer to someone with higher authority, to organize a task force or to form a study group when a simple decision would have sufficed. Followers want to know what their leader thinks about pertinent issues. They do not normally expect every decision to be without flaw, but they feel that they have the right to a timely decision from their leader.

HAS CLEAR GOALS AND VISION

It is rare to find an organization that has not articulated its goals, but it is less rare to find that a vision has not been promulgated throughout the organization. Goals are necessary indicators and benchmarks of progress, but a vision describes what the end result will be when we shall have achieved it.

In the area in which I grew up, virtually everyone had a dog. On occasions, one of these dogs would spy a rabbit and begin a chase through the neighborhood. Other dogs seeing the chase would join it. However, after a few minutes of running, the dogs would begin to drop out of the chase, one by one. There would always be one dog that continued the pursuit: that would be the dog that actually saw the rabbit. That dog would be running with a different motivation than the dogs that entered without commitment.

The same is true within an organization. When only the leadership has the vision, followers are likely to be less committed to the undetermined results than if there were a shared vision understood by all. Naturally, the vision may germinate in the mind of the leader, but is best developed through proper interaction with the followers.

GETS RID OF DEADWOOD

In most organizations, there are a few people who appear to have mastered the art of avoiding work. Generally, every one of their co-workers is aware of this tendency and they wonder why management has not discovered it. It can be very costly to one's leadership image if such matters are left unattended. The first reaction that some leaders have to rid the organization of dysfunctional personnel is to fire them. The flaw in this line of thinking is that if you fire your worst person, then the next worst person becomes your worst person. This practice could result in there being no one left except the leader who then becomes the worst person on staff. A more desirable practice is that of re-kindling the fire in the "dead wood" so that it again becomes live wood. Proper staff development, mentoring, coaching and counseling are some of the means through which one can restore the functionality of a given staff member.

COMPLAINS UPWARD

There are times when the leader in his or her trials wants a sympathetic listener with which to share his or her burdens. There are other times when the leader wants the followers to know that "it is not my fault" that things are not going as they should. A wise leader will avoid the temptation to ever use one's staff as such a sounding board. If you need to complain, always complain to someone who has the power and responsibility to act on your concern. Sharing your burden or difficulty with the staff can create some insecurity among the followers who would like to see you as the solution to their difficulties.

There will be issues for which you may not have the immediate solution. In such cases, let it be known that you are working with the proper authorities toward a solution and that you will keep all staff updated on the progress that is being made . The followers need to know that the leader will always act on their behalf to the best of his or her ability. Further, that the leader welcomes suggestions on how an issue might be favorably resolved.

HAS HIGH SELF-ESTEEM

Followers have a need to have pride in their leader. The leader who presents himself or herself in a respectful manner is more likely to receive respect from both followers and the public at large. High self-esteem should not be confused with arrogance. The latter is a selfish trait which generally manifests itself in the denigration of others. A psychologically healthy person has no need to be truculent with another human, particularly one who is in a following role. Followers are more likely to take pride in the self-control, confidence and composure of their leader.

SEES POTENTIAL IN OTHERS

Effective leaders surround themselves with persons who show potential for growth. One cannot always attract the most qualified personnel to join your team because highly qualified persons are in great demand and may choose not to work for you. A surer course of action is to select persons who have a proven track record in adjusting to new situations and growing into the roles that they have been called on to occupy. Look for successes that they have experienced in other walks of life, not limited to any specific job performance but in their management of life situations in general. An individual who has mastered the art of being successful can usually extrapolate from their life experience things that lead to success on the job.

REWARDS MERITORIOUS ACHIEVEMENT

It is a proven fact that we get more of whatever we reward. The leader who rewards undesirable behavior can expect to see more of that behavior. Leaders must be able to instill in followers the values that are prized by the organization of which they are a part. The effective leader consistently models these values and uses every opportunity to publicly reward those who practice them. The reward does not always have to be tangible. Simple recognition of one's exceptional contribution can be extremely gratifying to a follower. If bonuses are given, they should be based on superior performance and never on that which is designed to incur favor with the leader. Meritorious achievement always enhances the organization.

MANAGES CHANGE

Effective leaders can differentiate between "doing things better" and "doing better things". There are times when we need to improve on what we are doing. There are other times when we need to abandon a practice even if it has served us well in the past and employ newer approaches to achieving our objectives. Many people fear change because of the uncertainties associated with it. Others are reluctant to move out of their comfort zone and to try new approaches. The effective leader will provide the bridge for the followers to cross safely into new experiences, being careful not to incur unnecessary casualties along the way.

HAS A CONSISTENT MANAGEMENT STYLE

There are some advantages in knowing the leader's tendencies and general philosophy. When a leader has an erratic style, followers are frequently on edge. When the leader is consistent in rendering decisions based on what is known about a particular situation, trust in his or her judgment increases

MODELS DESIRABLE BEHAVIOR

An old adage often heard in the faith community is the one that says "I would rather see a sermon than to hear one." In other walks of life, this is equally true. The leader has an excellent opportunity to influence the environment by exhibiting the behavior that enhances the desirable ethos. When the leader demonstrates a belief in maintaining a certain standard through consistent action, others are more likely to follow that example.

PROMOTES POSITIVE THINKING

The effective leader seeks solutions rather that excuses, and exudes optimism rather than gloom and doom. A positive attitude is infectious and one person can change the total environment through the power of positive thinking. Ordinary people have achieved extraordinary things because they really believed that they could. The effective leader knows that the greatest motivator of people is their seeing the possibility of achieving their goal. Most of us need validation and affirmation as we move toward a goal. This can best come from the leader.

Beyond these cited traits, the effective leader will develop and project a basic leadership philosophy that will guide his or her behavior toward their followers. Some adopt an autocratic approach to leading in which the power of position plays a major role in how relationships are interpreted. This practice relies heavily on fear of repercussions for failing to please the leader. There are those who lose their ability to learn of their own weaknesses because of this practice. Subordinates are reluctant to share "bad news" with the leader, some of which may have led to the avoidance of mistakes. Fear may cause people to follow orders, but it rarely generates commitment to a mission.

A more reliable approach is that of consultative leadership. In this approach, the leader establishes parameters for the followers who are then able to operate with responsible autonomy within those parameters. This approach assumes that most people are capable of exercising self-direction when given definition of the area for which they are responsible.

At least four parameters must be predetermined for self-direction to have the greatest chance for success. One of these is policy. Every organization has policy which should be understood by all who are a part of the membership thereof. Members are then free to make decisions within the constraints of policy on their own volition.

A second parameter is that of limits of authority. Followers are entitled to know who has the authority to make or finalize decisions on matters that affect their daily activities. It is disheartening to have made a decision only to learn that this matter was beyond the scope of your authority. When it is clear in the beginning as to where one's authority begins and ends, such incidents can more easily be avoided.

A third parameter is that of philosophy. Every effective leader subscribes to a manner of doing things which it is hoped will permeate the organization. Each member of the organization must have an understanding of that philosophy since it becomes a part of the identity of the organization. An example of this can be seen in the growth of Wal-Mart into a major economic institution. Sam Walton, its founder had a philosophy that if a customer was seeking an article that they did not carry, they would add that article to their inventory. In following this pattern, they became the epitome of "one-stop shopping." Out of this disposition grew the concept of concern for the customer that is a part of the fabric of that organization.

Fourth, there must be a consideration of that which is acceptable in a certain culture. Many "good" practices that work well in one location may not be applicable in another setting. The effective leader must discern the feasibility of a given practice for a given situation.

Other parameters may include such factors as budget, political constraints, religious beliefs, tradition, rituals, and symbols, to name but a few. The greater the clarity that can be imparted regarding these matters, the more comfortable it becomes for members to exercise responsible autonomy.

Of the many theories on leadership that prevail in our times, one comment that has had a significant impact on the way that I think about the subject was given to us by Lao-tzu, a 6th century BC Chinese philosopher who was thought to have been the founder of Taoism. Of effective leadership, Lao-tzu remarked:

> *Of the best leaders, the people only know that they exist;*
> *The next best they love and praise;*
> *The next they fear;*
> *And the next they revile.*
> *When they do not command the people's faith*
> *Some will lose faith in them and they may resort to recriminations.*
> *But of the best, when their task is accomplished, their work done,*
> *The people will remark, "We have done it ourselves".*

Chapter IX

MAKING EFFECTIVE PRESENTATIONS

A RESEARCHER SEEKING TO LEARN THE greatest challenges faced by leaders in the nation's business community asked the question, "What aspect of your work do you find most challenging?" The great majority of the respondents answered that they most dreaded having to prepare and deliver an oral presentation. Many people have such a fear of having to speak before a group that they become physically affected. Some perspire profusely. Some develop nervous tremors, while others virtually lose their voices. It should not be surprising that the novice approaches this act with reservations. Yet, a great deal of our success rests upon our ability to deliver an effective presentation. In this chapter, we will offer some tips on making your presentations more effective.

Some of the tips referenced in the following pages were heretofore referenced in our publication written in 1987 titled "How to tell the Rest of the Story" and published through the North Carolina School Boards Association. However, there is here further elaboration on these points which we hope the reader will find helpful.

The most essential tool for making an effective presentation is that of a broad vocabulary. It should be noted that words are the currency of thought, and the greater your vocabulary the more easily you can transmit your thoughts to others. Inevitably, a person who is articulate is viewed by most people as being bright while an inarticulate person is generally viewed as being inept. Consequently, a major factor in forming ones public image is the ability to speak effectively.

PREPARING YOUR PRESENTATION

Material for a presentation is ever present. Professional speakers are always seeking bits of information that may someday be woven into a presentation. Compiling these bits of information, ideas, sayings, one-liners, and even memorable expressions from every day interaction with others can form a valuable reservoir to be used when you are ready to compose your speech. Every time you experience an original thought, you are generating material for a speech that you may one day make. Make it a habit to be in position to capture and retain those ideas for future reference. You may choose to take a tape recorder with you while driving alone on long trips. Have it handy so that when an idea enters your mind, you can speak it into the recorder. It may be that this idea will never occur to you again if it is lost.

When you are ready to prepare for a specific presentation, select the topic on which you are going to speak. Then go to your ideas file and pick out all the material that you have which relates to that topic. There is likely to be enough material there from which to form the nucleus of your presentation. From that point, it becomes easier to enrich your presentation by further research.

If time permits, prepare your topic outline well in advance of the time to make the presentation. This will allow you to live with the topic and as you do, new ideas and concepts related to the topic may enter your mind.

In preparing your presentation, be sensitive to the amount of information that you can effectively present and that your listeners can ingest it the allotted time. A typical audience will reject information overload thus nullifying what otherwise might have been an effective message.

You may increase your effectiveness by training yourself to be less dependent on a written text. You can do so by developing a list of mental cues, establishing them in a sequence and using your recall to summon each cue as needed. Organize your thoughts around each cue so well that the cue becomes a "spark plug" for a train of thought. Then put your concentration to work to hold your ideas together and to deliver them in the spirit that you feel them.

As you prepare your presentation, keep in mind that you cannot include everything that you know in one presentation. Prepare more that you could possibly present but use good judgment in knowing how much to use at a given time. Consider the following points as you develop your final script:

1. Format your presentation in independent modules of not more that five or six minutes duration. When given a specific amount of time in which to speak, select the most appropriate modules that will fit into that time frame, being careful to develop a flow that ties the thoughts neatly together. This method will help you to honor the time constraints which may be required of you.

2. Use real life stories and episodes to carry the points of your message. If it is true that one picture is worth a thousand words, then remember that one good story is worth a thousand pictures. The purpose of the story is to paint a word picture on the mind of the listener.

3. Develop your message so that it appeals to all the senses of the listener; hearing, sight, touch, smell, and taste. Naturally, not all the senses may be stimulated in every presentation, but when appropriately stimulated, they provoke greater identification with the message.

4. Control the level of intensity of your message. Molify highly emotional issues so as not to subject an audience with tension for long periods of time. One way of doing this is through the use of humor which will be further discussed later in this chapter.

5. Never insult your audience. Even in jest, one most be certain that listeners do not perceive that they have been disrespected. Perhaps the greatest insult is an insult to one's intelligence.

6. Avoid the use of profanity, vulgarity and sarcasm. Even when you use these as tools of emphasis, someone in you audience is going to be offended. When you offend, the rest of your presentation will be rejected.

USING HUMOR

The use of humor constitutes a valid and effective form of presentation. Humor can be the vehicle for carrying a very serious message. It can provide relief when appropriately interspersed within a particularly intense or sensitive presentation. It can be used as satire or to carry a subliminal message.

There are five potential dangers associated with the use of humor. However, there is a proper response to each of these dangers. Having experienced each of these, I have come to apply the following method of dealing with these situations.

1. The story that I tell may not be funny to the audience.

There are two basic ways to use humor. One is to tell funny stories; the other is to tell stories funny. No story is likely to have universal appeal, but if you are enough of a free spirit to tell stories funny, virtually any story will go over well. NEVER announce that you are going to tell a funny story. The critical element of humor is surprise. Never tell a story that will offend or embarrass your audience. What they find funny depends to a great extent on the setting, the rapport you have developed and the ethos of the group. Always be sensitive to different tastes, ages, religious differences, ethnic views and other areas of sensitivity. Will Rogers used to say that if there is no malice in your heart, there can be no malice in your humor. I agree, but would add that if your audience perceives that there is malice in your heart, it has the same consequence as if it were true.

2. People may focus on the humor and miss the real message.

Humor used well carries subtle but powerful messages. Often it makes distasteful messages more palatable to the listener. On balance, the gains outweigh the losses when humor is used wisely and well. Never tell a "joke" for the sake of trying to be funny during your presentation. If you can make a point that enriches your message or that vividly illustrates an abstract concept, your message is enhanced.

3. People EXPECT humor from you and lock you into telling stories out of context.

If you are an effective humorist, there will be certain stories that people come to identify with you. You may find that someone who has heard and enjoyed one of your stories wants to hear it again and will ask you to repeat it. However, the particular story that he or she requests may not fit into the presentation that you have prepared for this occasion. If that is the case, it is better to not force it in, but rather you might say to the requester, "I am glad that you liked that story and if I have the opportunity to do so, I will try to weave it into today's presentation." The key words are, "if I have the opportunity." Sometimes a good presentation gains latitude while in progress and the story may fit. If so, use it. If not, omit it. Your friend will understand after hearing the total message that his or her favorite story did not fit into this particular message.

4. People always want "new" stories.

Effective speakers are in many respects like effective entertainers. My all-time favorite entertainer, Johnny Mathis, has been performing two songs, "Chances Are" and "Wonderful, Wonderful" for more than fifty years. Yet, any fan that attends his concert still looks forward to hearing them again along with his newer material. In that same sense, an accomplished speaker may have certain standard lines which audiences look for and are disappointed if they do not hear. These well-worn stories used sparingly and in relevant context can still be effective. Try to keep a balance between the old and new, and remember that in every audience there is probably someone who is hearing your stories for the first time.

5. People with a no-nonsense attitude resent humor.

Remember that this is YOUR presentation. Do not allow two or three ill-tempered people to set the tone for you. If you establish the climate in which you work most effectively, you may even convert a poor audience into a more receptive audience.

As mentioned before, a good story must carry a message. In selecting the stories that you will incorporate into your presentation, determine first the point that you wish to make. Then select a story that makes that point. If the story is in sync with the rest of the message, it will not matter whether people find it to be funny. If they do, that is a bonus. If not, your message has not been compromised. A few of my favorites are shared here with the full knowledge that humor is largely dependent on the manner in which it is presented and that the written word can rarely deliver humor as does the spoken word, because humor is so highly dependent upon the rapport between the speaker and the hearers. In each instance, the point to be made is set forth first. Only in that context may the story carry the intended message.

KNOWLEDGE IS WHERE YOU FIND IT

In the small town in which I grew up, there were only three medical doctors. Whatever your ailment, your options rested with services of one of the three. A certain man developed some rather alarming reactions for which he went to see one of the doctors. The doctor asked him to relate the symptoms that he had been experiencing to which he answered, "I have a ringing in my ears, a roaring in my head, my eyes are bulging, and I can't get my breath." Upon hearing the symptoms, the doctor wrote him a prescription and sent him on his way. About two weeks later, the same symptoms returned, so he went to see a different doctor and was asked the same question, "What symptoms are you experiencing?" He gave the same response, "I have a ringing in my ears, a roaring in my head, my eyes are bulging, and I can't get my breath." The second doctor gave him a more in depth examination followed by a different prescription to try. After the passing of a few more days, the same symptoms returned, so he decided to try the third doctor.

When he reached the third doctor's office, he found that the word had spread of his condition and the doctor was prepared to give him the sad news. "I have studied the symptoms that you are having; the ringing in your head, the roaring in your ears, the bulging of your eyes and not being able to get your breath, and I regret to inform you that this condition is likely to be fatal. My advice is that you get your affairs in order."

The gentleman decided that if this was to be his fate, he would realize some of his unfulfilled desires. He had always wanted to travel, so he went out and bought a brand new car. He decided that he should have suitable traveling clothes, so he went to a first rate tailor and ordered a first rate outfit. Said he to the tailor, "I want a suit, coat size 42 long, pants 32 inseam, and a shirt with sleeves 35 inches and collar 15 and a half." The tailor responded that he usually measured his clients for their dimensions and proceeded to do so. After having so done, he informed his customer that most of his measurements were just as he had described. However, the neck measurement should have been 16 and a half, not 15 and a half. The man responded, "I have always worn a 15 and a half and that is what I want you to make." The tailor replied, "If that is what you want, I will make it as you say, but I warn you that as soon as you put it on and button the collar, you are going to have a ringing in your head, a roaring in your ears, your eyes are going to bulge and you won't be able to get your breath."

SMART PEOPLE CAN MAKE MISTAKES, TOO

In the early days of air travel, it was common for travelers to rely on parachutes as a refuge if a plane were to malfunction. On an occasion, three very important officials were traveling on a small plane to attend an important meeting in the mountains of North Carolina. An intern of one of the officials asked to go along so that he might go back packing while the officials were conducting their business. His wish was granted, so the four of them along with the pilot boarded the plane and took of toward their destination.

A short way into the flight, the pilot heard a disturbing sound in the plane's engine and announced to the travelers, "Gentlemen, I have some disturbing news. We are experiencing engine trouble, and we may have to abandon the plane." The leader of the officials looked into the parachute storage space and discovered that there was not a chute for each person on the plane, so he said to the others, "There are not enough parachutes to go around, so since I am essential to our mission, I will take the first one and jump to safety. You can decide who will not have a parachute after I have jumped." Having made that decision, he proceeded to jump from the small plane.

The remaining passengers began to talk among themselves as to who would use the rest of the parachutes and who would trust his fate without one, when the young intern spoke up. "Gentlemen, I wouldn't worry about that. There are plenty of parachutes left since the leader who jumped was wearing my back pack."

IMPATIENCE HAS ITS CONSEQUENCES

Two men were hiking on a beautiful trail in the park. One of them was given to stammering in his speech and the other was rather intolerant of his difficulty. As they were walking, they passed a very attractive lady who too was out for a walk. The stammerer began "Ma-ma-man, d-d-d-did you s-s-s-see that p-p-p pretty girl?" The friend replied, "Where?" The stammerer replied, "S-s-s-she's gone now." A few minutes later, the stammerer began again, "Ma-ma-man, d-d-d-did you s-s-see what I j-j-just s-s-saw?" His friend, looking around quickly asked again, "Where?" to which the stammerer replied, "S-s-she's g-g-gone, too." By now, the impatient friend was determined to not engage further in this type of interaction, so when the stammerer began again, "D-d-did you s-s-see—"his friend interrupted him saying, "Man, I saw it." The stammerer responded, "W-w-well, if you s-s-saw it, wh-wh-why d-d-did you step in it?"

SOMETIMES, WE DON'T KNOW WHAT WE DON'T KNOW

A church was holding its business meeting and a discussion of the annual budget was the agenda item. A member stood to be recognized and offered a motion that the church purchase a chandelier for the sanctuary. Near the back of the church sat a man who was totally exercised over this notion and became so distracting with his objecting that the presider asked if he would stand and give reasons for his objections

The objector replied, "I object for three reasons, First, if we vote to get one, we couldn't order it because none of us knows how to spell it; secondly, if we had one, no one in here knows how to play it, and most importantly, if we are going to spend some money, we ought to put some lights in this church."

These are but a few examples of humor that may be used to carry a point. Neither of these examples would likely appeal to a listener if presented out of context, but when used to make a point, they can add interest and may help with the retention of the intended message.

In this writing, only a few of the specifics of making effective presentations have been addressed. Others will occur to you as you become more experienced in public speaking .In summary, the vital elements to remember are to prepare well, to have a positive attitude toward your work and toward your audience, and to be yourself. The best presenters do not simply give speeches; they give themselves.

Chapter X

ORDER, CONTROL, AND
VALUES = DISCIPLINE

EDUCATORS KNOW THAT A LEARNING atmosphere can be greatly enhanced by order in a school. To assure that order will prevail, there must be an effective system or means to control behavior.

Discipline is defined as "training that corrects, molds, or perfects the mental faculties or moral faculties." This implies that mere control of pupils is not discipline in the finest state, but that discipline must aim toward the perfection of lasting values and permanent qualities which will be the frame of reference for all future behavior.

Some Factors that Influence Pupil Behavior

If school personnel are to effectively channel the behavior of pupils, they must have some knowledge of the factors which influence the behavioral trends of today's youth. Some basic knowledge of human sociology is helpful in interpreting the individual student's behavior.

Discipline problems are the natural and logical results of the breaking down of relationships between and among people. Teachers should be aware of the existence of certain factors in our social structure which comprise natural barriers to the learning process and human interaction. We are socially grouped into different division according to such factors as geographical residence, political philosophy, economic possessions, age and race. When making the designation of these divisions, status is often assigned. For example, north is higher than south, urban is higher than rural, rich is higher than poor, white is higher than black, and old is higher than young in terms of status. The fact that such division and status positions exist make it likely that the most natural position for members of opposite groups to take would be adversarial positions.

The barrier of age has been often referred to as the "generation gap." The solution of bridging the gap may be found in understanding some of the causes of its existence.

Age is a restrictive barrier in the minds of youth. They tend to view the status of adults with envy and resentment. Their natural reaction is to "put down" the adult image; that is, to label the image so negatively as to assure ample defense against its glamour. The paradox here is that while rejecting the adult image overtly, the same youth may be striving to imitate that image.

Self-concept is frequently consistent with the status assignment imposed by the barriers mentioned earlier. Students' images of others are also consistent with the perceived assigned status of others. Thus the basis for the relationship between persons emerges from the perspective in which they view themselves in relation to others in keeping with status positions. For example, suppose that the teacher is white, middle-class, urban and old and the student is black, low-class, rural and young. There are present in this relationship four natural barriers which must be realized and overcome before learning can receive priority. The more opposite characteristics one adds to this list, the more deterrents to the learning process are in evidence. Compatibility can ensue more naturally if the teacher becomes aware of the presence of those barriers and works actively toward the elimination of them.

Learned Values Result from Experience

Experience is the basis for our values. For many children, the school provides their only opportunity to learn a system of positive values. The environment in which economically deprived children live may foster a set of values in a completely different perspective from that of the child who is the product of an affluent community. A case in point is the formation of attitudes toward work.

To the child of middle-class parents, "work" may denote a condition of arising in the morning, having a warm shower, hot breakfast, dressing neatly, and heading for the office, plant or school to return early in the evening, enjoy a leisurely meal and relax or recreate. To the child of low economic class parents, work may denote awaking before sunrise, being away from home far into the evening, coming home too tired to be attentive to either family needs or living conditions and deriving no self-gratification and little financial reward from one's efforts. It is easy to see why one of these conditions inspires initiative while the other begets disdain for "work."

When children are reared in an atmosphere of economic instability and their needs of subsistence must frequently go unsatisfied, their goals are likely to be short-ranged and materialistic. Children have difficulty focusing their attention on such objectives as career goals and worthy adult citizenship when faced with the question of whether they will have food for today's dinner or shoes to wear to school tomorrow.

The pupil who is loud and boisterous may be the product of an environment where loudness is essential for effective communication. Children who live next to the railroad tracks, an interstate highway or an industrial plant learn to compete with noise. They also learn to "tune out" unwanted sounds, which may include the lecture of a classroom teacher or the pleadings of a parent.

Another value which many pupils lack is that of meeting strict requirements of time. Here again the economic factor is an influence. When people have nothing of importance to do day after day, time has little importance to them. The carryover of this attitude from adults to children is evident among economically disadvantaged youth, resulting in their often being late for school and frequently being absent for trivial reasons.

Promptness may be encouraged by assigning responsibility to these pupils. They will usually respond to purpose, but may not have a complete transformation overnight. Time and reinforcement are both necessary to complete the process.

These are a few illustrations of the pattern by which experiences shape values and ultimately determine behavior.

Peer Group Approval

One of the most dynamic forces influencing student behavior is peer group approval. Modes of dress, language usage, fads, and slogans are standardized on this factor.

Since youths' self-image is that of having categorical subservient status, inner-group identity tends to develop. Common habits and customs must be adopted for the purpose of maintaining acceptable membership in the group. Many young people are hereby made social captives, indulging in acts they neither enjoy nor condone.

To deal effectively with discipline problems which are motivated by the desire for approval of peer groups, adults must recognize that forcefulness on their part may be the desired response. Force tends to polarize the positions of the two age groups and may make a "martyr" of the offender.

Many overt acts of pupil behavior are symptomatic of deeply rooted attitudes based on family and peer group experiences. This is especially true with respect to reactions to racial labels and symbols. The disruptions to school programs which grow out of racial reactions usually defy any rationale. Classroom confrontations between pupils of different races place the educators in a precarious position. They must decide whether it is feasible to remove the participants in disruptions from the school setting at the price of depriving them of further educational opportunities, or to attempt the longer and more delicate task of influencing attitudes. Many educators feel that attitudes are basically developed and reinforced by the home and that it is a waste of time to try to change them. Experience shows, however, that students want the acceptance of their school community, including the teachers. It may be worth the time and effort to give it a try.

SOME SPECIFIC APPLICATIONS OF DISCIPLINARY ACTION

Matters involving routine discipline are expected to occur in any school and should be handled by the teacher nearest to the problem at the time of its occurrence. Infractions of a serious nature should be referred to the principal. In either case, prevention is more beneficial to all concerned than is punishment after the act.

Define Areas of Unacceptable Behavior

Since the terms "right" and "wrong" are relative terms, they serve little purpose as a basis for establishing guidelines for student behavior. Pupils can defend in their own minds almost any act we might label as wrong or bad by pointing to some respectable person who does it. There may also be conflicting opinions between home and school as to what is good or bad.

A workable alternative to labeling as "bad" is categorizing behavior as *acceptable* and *unacceptable*. The end objective remains the same; that the pattern of behavior will be modified. However, the stimulus is a much more positive one and desirable results are more likely to occur. To look at a specific point, children whose parents are frequent imbibers of alcoholic beverages cannot condemn the act of drinking as being bad without also condemning their own parents. However, the term "acceptable" restricts judgment to those immediate areas over which the school has jurisdiction. This includes the student's behavior and excludes that of the parent. Children can then see that the school is concerned about their habits and not necessarily being critical of persons outside the school.

This same principle holds true with regard to a wide range of acts including smoking, the use of profanity, cheating, lying and stealing, fighting, untidiness, rudeness and many others. The principle of the unacceptability of these must be sold to the student body to the extent that they begin to remind each other to avoid the performing of such acts.

Avoid Embarrassing Students

The teacher and administrator must be constantly aware of the fact that young people are very sensitive to their status in society. They are beginning at the junior high school age to become deeply concerned with the image which their peers may have of them and the desire for peer group approval becomes a dominant factor in influencing pupil behavior.

Adults should be especially careful to avoid personal references to pupils in this age group. The pupils should be made to see the act as separate and apart from the person. The act is rejected, not the children. The children discern that they must discontinue this act so they can maintain their acceptability. This becomes a positive incentive to do that which is more the norm of behavior in this setting.

This approach is more effective if it can be done with the individual in privacy. If several students are guilty of the same violation, there is a great temptation to deal with them as a group and there are occasions which may necessitate group council. However, individual conferences usually affect pupils more in that a feeling of personal worth is gained from having had the personal attention of someone in authority.

Avoid "Baiting" Students

Teachers should be constantly aware of the effect their mannerisms have on pupils. If personal issues are injected into the school setting, personal idiosyncrasies may become a deterrent to the learning process.

Students should never be placed in the position of feeling that they have nothing further to lose. When a teacher assigns grades to a pupil which are so low that they cannot possibly be offset within the scope of the term, the reward of being promoted ceases to be an incentive, and the pupils may lose their dedication. They may also transfer their energy from constructive to disruptive practices.

It is advisable that, as far as possible, the grading process should be used to reflect only the measurable aspect of academic achievement. If the practice of lowering grades is used to enforce discipline, some of the validity of their significance is lost.

Avoid Debating with Students

Teachers, having made decisions, should not degrade themselves by engaging in debate with pupils regarding the merits of their decisions. It is healthy to hear the opinions of the students on matters affecting their welfare, but nothing is to be gained from arguing a point. If the stand which the teacher has taken is a good and fair one, it will not need to be defended to the student. If it is a poor or unfair decision, the teacher will do well to take the initiative to change it as soon as he/she recognizes its shortcomings.

Avoid Threats to Pupils

The wise teacher will always leave room for discussion on issues. Even after an issue is closed, there should be some graceful recourse by which the final decision may be modified.

Teachers should not anticipate the disposition the principal will make of a disciplinary issue. Before having allowed the principal to react to information surrounding an issue, teachers sometimes predict to pupils that the "principal should expel you" or some like form of punishment. Should the principal reach some other decision after having weighed the issues, he/she will probably alienate the teacher. The teacher's role should be to present the issues to the principal who in turn should make the decision on the basis of the information presented and whatever factors are involved. Teachers should remember that the principle of justice which holds that the accused must be deemed innocent until guilt is established holds equally true in the school.

Avoid Conflicting Policy

The code of behavior for a school should be administered uniformly throughout the school. Acts prohibited in one classroom and tolerated in another cause a general breakdown in discipline. For instance, if teacher A allows gum chewing in class and teacher B prohibits it; one wonders if the rules were not arbitrarily made by teacher B.

Areas in which final authority rests with the teacher should be defined in the school policy guide. Matters not covered in these areas which involve serious offenses should be called to the principal's attention. Since principals are the officially responsible officers of the school; they need to be appraised of matters of serious implications so that they can relate them in proper prospective to all individuals concerned.

Students expect to have some authority exerted over their behavior. Teachers or principals who fail to recognize this fact may not win the respect of their pupils. Teachers should use their own authority in as many situations as possible. The best place for solving problems of discipline is at the classroom level. When a pupil has to be taken to the principal, this represents a different level of disciplinary action with more social implications. If the case goes all the way to the superintendent, this involves yet another set of social implications; and if it must be acted on by the board of education, it may have reached dramatic proportions. Obviously, the hope is that most issues which arise in the school will be solved by teachers working directly with their students.

Should teachers find themselves to be in error in dealing with students, they should not be reluctant to admit their mistakes. They will suffer no loss of prestige from such an admission. The best time to right an injustice is just as soon as it is discovered. Delay usually results in defensiveness rather than corrective action.

Conclusions

It seems needless to say that none of the measures discussed here can guarantee that good behavior will result from their application. There is, however, strong evidence to support the position that if students are expected to behave well and if "acceptable behavior" is identified and shared as a mutual goal by parents, students, teachers and other school officials, it will be achieved.